RUFINUS

A COMMENTARY ON
THE APOSTLES' CREED

COMMENTARIUS IN SYMBOLUM APOSTOLORUM

ANCIENT CHRISTIAN WRITERS

THE WORKS OF THE FATHERS IN TRANSLATION

EDITED BY

JOHANNES QUASTEN, S. T. D.
Catholic University of America
Washington, D.C.

JOSEPH C. PLUMPE, Ph.D
Pontifical College Josephinum
Worthington, O.

No. 20

RUFINUS

A COMMENTARY
ON THE APOSTLES' CREED

TRANSLATED AND ANNOTATED

BY

J. N. D. KELLY, D.D. (Oxon)
Principal
St. Edmund Hall, Oxford

NEWMAN PRESS

New York, N.Y./Ramsey, N.J.

Nihil Obstat:
> J. Quasten
> > *Cens. Dep.*

Imprimatur:
> Patricius A. O'Boyle, D.D.
> > *Archiep. Washingtonen*
> > > *die 19 Maii 1954*

Library of Congress
Catalog Card Number: 78-62468

ISBN: 0-8091-0257-9

PUBLISHED BY PAULIST PRESS
Editorial Office: 1865 Broadway, New York, N.Y. 10023
Business Office: 545 Island Road, Ramsey, N.J. 07446

PRINTED AND BOUND IN THE UNITED STATES OF AMERICA

CONTENTS

RUFINUS

A COMMENTARY ON
THE APOSTLES' CREED

COMMENTARIUS IN SYMBOLUM APOSTOLORUM

INTRODUCTION

1. THE AUTHOR

Tyrannius Rufinus was born about A.D. 345 in the small North Italian town of Concordia, at the head of the Adriatic, not far to the west of Aquileia.[1] The son of Christian parents, he was sent as a youth to Rome to complete his education, and among the fellow students with whom he speedily formed ties was another northerner of about the same age, Jerome, from Stridon in Dalmatia. Probably in 368, the year of St. Jerome's departure from the capital for 'the semi-barbarous banks of the Rhine,'[2] Rufinus returned to northern Italy, attaching himself to a community of ascetics which had sprung up at Aquileia under the inspiration of the exiled St. Athanasius during his sojourn there about 345. Within a year or two he was formally received into the Church, being baptized by the priest Chromatius who was later to become Bishop of Aquileia. Meanwhile he maintained friendly relations with St. Jerome, who seems to have been a frequent visitor to the monastic house. But this phase of his life, so potent in planting in him the vision of ascetic perfection, was not destined to last long. About 372 St. Jerome suddenly broke away from the group, setting out on a pilgrimage which took him through Thrace, Bithynia, and Pontus, and eventually to Syria. Rufinus, too, seized with a similar longing to visit the authentic home of monasticism, embarked on a journey to Alexandria and Egypt.

Somewhere about this time Rufinus's fortunes became

linked with those of another devout seeker after the higher spiritual life, the rich and noble Roman widow known as Melania the Elder.[3] After a six months' visit to the desert fathers of Nitria, in Lower Egypt,[4] we find him settled with her at Alexandria, where he attended the lectures of Didymus the Blind and made the acquaintance of the works of Origen. During the Arian persecution which flared up after St. Athanasius's death in 373, he apparently suffered imprisonment and exile. In the meantime Melania had betaken herself to Palestine, and had established a community of virgins in Jerusalem on the Mount of Olives. Here Rufinus rejoined her, probably in 380, founding a community for men in close proximity to her convent. For the next eighteen years they laboured together, entertaining bishops, monks, and virgins with lavish hospitality, and pursuing literary studies as well as supervising their religious houses.[5] It was during this period, about the year 390, that Rufinus received ordination to the priesthood, probably at the hands of John, the Bishop of Jerusalem.

Up to this point Rufinus had led an inconspicuous, though busy life, with his thoughts dominated by the dream of monastic dedication and self-renunciation. Now he found himself thrown into the bitterly conducted quarrel about Origen and the orthodoxy of his theology, and incidentally became an author. The first rift between himself and his boyhood friend St. Jerome dates back to 393, when a zealot named Atarbius charged them both with the heresy (for such it was becoming in certain strict circles) of Origenism. While St. Jerome was prepared to offer formal abjuration of the errors alleged, Rufinus declined to make any defence. Much more serious was the attack which, a little later, St. Epiphanius launched against Rufinus's friend, Bishop John of Jerusalem. Rufinus rushed to John's support, while St. Jerome sided with the aged and stiffly conservative St. Epiphanius. A reconciliation was nevertheless patched up, and complete amity had been restored between them when Rufinus set sail for the West in 397. Once in Italy, however, Rufinus took up the task of translating Greek theological writings into Latin, and at the request of the erudite philosopher Macarius produced a Latin version of Origen's *De principiis*. In view of the anti-Origenistic atmosphere of the times this was a tactless move, but he made matters much worse by claiming that he had adhered to St. Jerome's methods, and by attempting to whitewash Origen with the plea that the heretical blemishes disfiguring his works were the result of interpolation. St. Jerome's reaction was typically violent, and a chasm yawned between the two old friends which all the efforts of well-wishers proved powerless to bridge. In addition to his private dispute with St. Jerome, Rufinus now found himself faced with public doubts as to his orthodoxy, and he was obliged to address a reasoned defence of his position to the reigning Pope, Anastasius. Worse still, the abuse and vituperation with which St. Jerome continued to belabour him till his death were to darken his reputation for succeeding centuries.[6]

About 398 Rufinus returned to Aquileia, where the spiritual guide of his youth, Chromatius, now occupied the see. Here he embarked on a period of strenuous literary activity, producing (in addition to controversial manifestos) a series of translations of Greek ecclesiastical authors, not excluding Origen, as well as original works of his own. It was probably a happy, as well as a creative, interlude in his career. He enjoyed the friendship and confidence of such men as Bishop Gaudentius of Brescia and St. Paulinus of Nola, as well as of other Church leaders in the region of

Venetia and Milan. The outstanding figure of the age, St. Augustine of Hippo, never faltered in his esteem of him, and refused to take sides in the acrimonious quarrel with St. Jerome.[7] But in 407 Chromatius died, and Rufinus took his final leave of Aquileia, making for Rome and the monastery at Pinetum, near the modern Terracina, over which his friend Ursacius presided as abbot. Political upheavals and the military invasion of the Goths did not make North Italy a comfortable locality for an aging man; and it is possible that his thoughts were turning once again in the direction of Jerusalem. His intended route required him to cross over to Africa by Sicily, and he was on the island, with Melania the Younger (the grand-daughter of his sometime spiritual companion) and her husband Pinianus, when Alaric's hordes moved southwards after the sack of Rome. There is a moving passage in the preface to his translation of Origen's *Homilies on Numbers*, describing how, looking across the straits towards Italy, he had witnessed the burning of Rhegium (Reggio) by the barbarians.[8] That was in September, 410: he was then suffering badly from eye-trouble, and shortly afterwards he died. A malicious sentence of St. Jerome's, prefixed to his *Commentary on Ezechiel* written in 411, establishes the date, and confirms that Sicily was his burial place.[9]

Though in keeping with his fiery temperament, St. Jerome's insistence on carrying the quarrel beyond the grave was in every way unfortunate. Intellectually Rufinus was no match for him; but he was a good man, and he certainly conducted his side of the controversy with more dignity and Christian tact than his hot-blooded opponent. The outline of his personality is lost behind his writings, but seems to have been humble-minded and retiring, with the intense ascetical bias which was typical of the age. He had the resolution and firmness of character to stand up for his principles when they were attacked; and, with the unhappy exception of St. Jerome, it is remarkable how readily he won and retained the affection of his Christian contemporaries.

2. THE COMMENTARY ON THE APOSTLES' CREED

Rufinus cannot be acclaimed as one of the great Christian writers of the fourth century. Belonging to the epoch which produced such giants as St. Ambrose and St. Augustine (to mention only the West), he would have been the first to admit the mediocrity of his stature. Nevertheless, despite inevitable limitations, his literary achievement ought not to be underrated. The great body of his writings consisted of translations, and on these his reputation as an author must principally rest. His translations of Origen are particularly important, including as they do the *De principiis* and the commentaries on Canticles and Romans, as well as a host of homilies. In addition, he published versions of Eusebius's *Ecclesiastical History*, St. Basil's *Regulae* and a number of his sermons, nine orations of St. Gregory Nazianzen, the *Historia monachorum*, and several other works. As a translator he followed principles which would not gain acceptance today. Often his renderings were loose paraphrases or even shortened adaptations, and in the case of Origen he did not scruple to modify or suppress passages which he mistakenly supposed to have suffered alteration or interpolation at unorthodox hands.[10] It would be unfair to judge him, however, by standards which may be *de rigeur* in the twentieth century, but which were not so strictly imposed in the fourth and fifth. On the positive side, the service he rendered to the Church by making Eastern ascetical and theological developments accessible to the Latin-speaking West must on any reckoning be acknowledged to have been substantial.

The original writings standing to his credit are singularly few—the *Apology to Anastasius*, the *Apology against Jerome*, two books[11] continuing the narrative of Eusebius's *Ecclesiastical History* from 325 to 395, two books *De benedictionibus patriarcharum*, and some letters and commentaries which have not survived. To this list must be added the *Commentarius in symbolum Apostolorum* (otherwise described as *Expositio symboli Apostolorum*), which is perhaps the most important of all his works, and which certainly was to exercise a widespread influence. In the Middle Ages it was generally handed down under the name either of St. Cyprian or, ironically enough, of St. Jerome, a circumstance which may account for the popularity it enjoyed in spite of the cloud overhanging Rufinus. That he was in fact its true author admits of no reasonable doubt. Its stylistic and doctrinal affinities with his other writings are transparent, and there is early testimony to his having written about the creed. John Cassian,[12] for example, made explicit reference to an *Expositio symboli* by Rufinus, following it up with a textually exact quotation from chapter 13. Less than half a century after Rufinus's death, Gennadius of Marseilles noted[13] that 'by his own efforts . . . this same Rufinus produced an exposition of the creed in comparison with which the attempts of others scarcely count as expositions at all.'

The *Commentarius* is addressed to a certain Bishop Laurentius: his rank may be deduced from the respectful title 'Papa' which Rufinus applied to him. He it was at whose request the little work was undertaken. Nothing further is known of his identity. The conjecture of J. Fontanini[14] that he was bishop of Concordia, Rufinus's birthplace, was only a guess, and the fact that there is no definite record of any occupant of that see prior to Clarissimus (A.D. 578), perhaps militates against it. Even less plausible is D. Vallarsi's suggestion[15] that 'Laurenti' in the manuscripts may be a misreading for 'Gaudenti.' It is true that Gaudentius, the contemporary bishop of Brescia, belonged to Rufinus's circle of personal friends, and that the latter dedicated his translation of the Pseudo-Clementine *Recognitions* to him. But, quite apart from the difficulty of explaining the corruption of such an obvious and easy reading as 'Gaudenti' into the enigmatical 'Laurenti,' there seems no justification for assuming that the list of Rufinus's acquaintances is exhaustively known to us.

It is usual to date the *Commentarius* round about the year 404. The text of the treatise itself contains no pointer to any particular epoch, but the close similarity between the discussion of the resurrection body given in chapter 43 and the treatment of the same theme in his two *Apologies*[16] has been taken to imply that it must be posterior to them. The *Apologia ad Anastasium* is ascribed to 400, and the *Apologia in Hieronymum* to 401. If these dates are correct, and if the argument founded on them is trustworthy, the book may well have been composed two or three years earlier than 404. But anything approaching an exact dating is excluded by the lack of precise evidence.

The particular literary *genre* to which Rufinus's essay belongs was by no means unfamiliar to his contemporaries. He himself remarked, in his opening paragraphs, that he had had forerunners in the same field. Half a century previously, in 347 or 348,[17] St. Cyril of Jerusalem had delivered his famous *Catechetical Lectures*. Thirteen of these (in addition to a *Procatachesis*, there were twenty-three *Cate-cheses* proper, and the thirteen in question are nos. 6–18) were based on the successive articles of the Jerusalem creed, which in effect they paraphrased and expounded at great length. These lectures were widely read, and set a model to subsequent writers, such as Gelasius of Caesarea (✠395), who included an 'Interpretation of the Creed'[18] in the ninth tractate of a general introduction to Christian doctrine. The fifth of the six *Libelli instructionis*[19] published by Niceta, bishop of Remesiana in the latter decades of the fourth century, and, like Rufinus, a close friend of St. Paulinus of Nola, also consisted of an exposition of the baptismal creed for the benefit of catechumens. Yet another example is the *Explanatio symboli ad initiandos*,[20] a tract not dissimilar to Rufinus's, though much briefer and of a more limited scope, which should probably be regarded as notes of a lecture delivered by St. Ambrose to candidates for baptism. St. Augustine, too, when he was still only a priest, addressed a gathering of bishops at Hippo on the Catholic faith, using the baptismal creed as the framework of his discourse, and publishing it under the title *De fide et symbolo*.[21] The surviving collection of his Sermons also contains four addresses[22] to candidates for baptism, three preached when the baptismal creed was handed out to them (the *traditio symboli*), and the fourth on the occasion of their solemn rehearsal of it before the bishop (the *redditio symboli*). All four are succinct theological expositions of the creed in language adapted to the intellectual level of his audience.

As it stands, Rufinus's treatise reads smoothly and freshly, and has all the air of being an original work. Though by no means so brilliant with his pen as his relentless critic St. Jerome, Rufinus wrote a skilful and sometimes attractive style, and he had the ability to leave his personal imprint on whatever material he handled. Yet it is plain that, even in the *Commentarius*, he did not rely exclusively on his own invention. In the nature of the case, since he was expounding the creed for converts and others undergoing instruction, he drew largely on the Church's stock of catechetical commonplaces. Over and above that, there were at least two literary sources which he had made his own and from which he deliberately borrowed. One was the *Oratio catechetica* of St. Gregory of Nyssa, a reasoned defence of the main doctrines of Christianity against heretics, Jews, and pagans, written somewhat prior to 385. The influence of chapters 32 and 6 of this work is discernible in chapters 14 and 15 of Rufinus's essay,[23] and there can be little doubt that its teaching lies behind other sections as well. Much more striking and all-pervasive, however, was the impact of St. Cyril's *Catechetical Lectures*. No source, it has recently been pointed out,[24] has so far been discovered for the first thirteen and the last three chapters of the *Commentarius*, but the remainder of the work is largely based on *Catecheses* 13–18. The measure of its dependence should become vividly and convincingly apparent to the reader as he studies the text with the aid of the appended notes. Here it is sufficient to observe that, while Rufinus often makes fresh points and appeals to illustrations of his own choosing, he is indebted to St. Cyril for the sequence and framework of his exposition, for a great proportion of his arguments, and for the majority of his Scriptural quotations. It would not be unfair to describe his treatise, or at any rate the main body of it, as a rather free, drastically abbreviated presentation in Latin of St. Cyril's teaching in the *Catechetical Lectures*.

3. THE BAPTISMAL CREED

For theologian and general reader alike the chief interest of Rufinus's treatise must lie in the glimpse it allows of popular Christian propaganda at the beginning of the fifth century. The audience he envisaged, as he repeatedly emphasized, consisted of persons under instruction for the sacraments. His essay was to be a sort of handbook or guide elucidating and justifying the creed to which they would be expected to pledge their allegiance at their baptism. That these were people of some education and cultural background seems to be implied by the level of his discussion and argument. For the modern student it is fascinating to follow his exposition, noticing the kind of doubts and errors he felt entitled to anticipate, and the kind of considerations he judged it reasonable to deploy against them. On balance the verdict must be that Rufinus was a competent teacher, and that the case for Christianity which he set before his charges was a carefully reasoned and intellectually respectable one.

For the specialist, with his narrower interests, the *Commentarius* has unique importance because of the testimony it bears to the evolution of credal forms. The knowledge we possess of creeds, both Western and Eastern, in the early centuries is disappointingly meagre. So far as Eastern creeds are concerned, it is fortunate that Eusebius of Caesarea felt constrained, in justification of his conduct at the Council of Nicaea, to dispatch a lengthy letter to the Caesarean church containing, among other things, a verbatim citation of the local baptismal creed.[25] Since he prefaced it with the assurance that this was the formulary which had been used for his own instruction and baptism, it is reasonable to trace its origin well back into the third century. From St. Cyril's *Catechetical Lectures* it is possible to reconstruct, with some measure of confidence and exactitude, the text of the baptismal creed of Jerusalem in the second generation of the fourth century.[26] The situation as regards the West is hardly more favourable. It is true that the *Apostolic Tradition* of St. Hippolytus, written towards the close of the pontificate of Pope Zephyrinus (198–217), contains an account of the baptismal rite, and that this includes the three credal questions, in Greek in the original, which were put to candidates at the critical moment of their threefold immersion.[27] From these an interrogative creed can be pieced together which was undoubtedly current at Rome when St. Hippolytus wrote, and which is consequently of extraordinary importance. At the beginning of the third century, however, the liturgy was still fluid, and there is no reason for supposing that a single official form had already been canonized, much less had secured a monopoly, at Rome. Apart from this striking but solitary witness, and a few fragmentary excerpts quoted by Tertullian and St. Cyprian, Western creeds are shrouded in almost complete darkness until the times of Niceta of Remesiana, St. Augustine, and Rufinus.

The part played by Rufinus's treatise in dissipating this darkness cannot be exaggerated. It provides precious, indispensable material for reconstituting the texts of two important local creeds (one of them of much more than local significance), that of Aquileia and that of Rome. This becomes obvious to anyone who examines Rufinus's procedure. The whole purpose of his book, as he explained in the introductory sections, was to expound what he called 'the Apostles' symbol.' He was convinced, rightly or wrongly, that before departing from Jerusalem on their several missionary journeys the twelve Apostles had drafted an agreed summary of the faith, each of them contributing one article. The resulting composition was for him 'the Apostles' symbol,' and it was this that he proposed to expound. He was further convinced, however, that, while the apostolic summary of the faith had undergone modifications in various local churches, mainly through the necessity of combating heresy, it had been preserved intact, in its pristine shape, at Rome. One reason for this, he thought, was the fortunate immunity of Rome from heresies, while a second was the Roman liturgical custom which caused the creed to be rehearsed at baptism in a uniquely public fashion, thereby safeguarding it from interpolation.[28] In the light of these ideas his natural course, one might have assumed, would have been to comment, clause by clause, on the Roman creed. Instead, for the pious reason that it was the creed of his own baptism, he selected the Aquileian formulary as the basis of his disquisition. At the same time he adhered to his original design of expounding the Apostles' (that is, in effect, the Roman) creed by drawing his readers' attention to any features of the Aquileian text which differed significantly from the Roman.

It was James Ussher,[29] the Anglican archbishop of Armagh, who in 1647 first drew the inference that Rufinus was a witness to the contemporary Roman creed as well as to the creed of his local church. In addition, he thought himself able to trace the Roman creed more than half a century back by pointing out that the theological apologia which Marcellus of Ancyra, the over-zealous exponent of Nicene orthodoxy whom the Eusebian party had extruded from his see, submitted in 340 to Pope Julius I contained a brief credal formula[30] which was substantially identical with Rufinus's version of the Apostolicum. The manifest implication, as it seemed to Ussher, was that Marcellus, as the final and absolutely unimpeachable proof of his orthodoxy, was in effect adducing his acceptance of the pope's own creed. With only isolated and, it may be held, inadequately grounded expressions of misgiving,[31] Ussher's identification has been universally admitted to be correct down to the present day.

For the convenience of readers the texts of the Aquileian and the Roman creeds probably familiar to Rufinus are printed below. As it was not part of Rufinus's purpose to underline minutiae of word-order, grammar, etc., the latter text has been checked by certain ancient MSS which contain it.[32]

AQUILEIA

Credo in Deo Patre omnipotente invisibili et impassibili;	I believe in God the Father almighty, invisible and impassible;
Et in Christo Iesu, unico Filio eius, Domino nostro,	And in Christ Jesus, His only Son, our Lord,
qui natus est de Spiritu sancto ex Maria Virgine,	Who was born by the Holy Spirit from the Virgin Mary,
crucifixus sub Pontio Pilato et sepultus,	crucified under Pontius Pilate and buried,
descendit ad inferna,	He descended to hell,
tertia die resurrexit a mortuis,	on the third day He rose again from the dead,
ascendit ad caelos,	He ascended to heaven,
sedet ad dexteram Patris,	He sits at the Father's right hand,
inde venturus est iudicare vivos et mortuos;	thence He will come to judge living and dead;
Et in Spiritu sancto, sanctam ecclesiam, remissionem peccatorum, huius carnis resurrectionem.	And in the Holy Spirit, the Holy Church, the remission of sins, the resurrection of this flesh.

ROME

Credo in Deum Patrem omnipotentem;	I believe in God the Father almighty;

Et in Christum Iesum, Filium	And in Christ Jesus, His only
eius unicum, Dominum nostrum,	Son, our Lord,
qui natus est de Spiritu sancto	Who was born from the
et Maria Virgine,	Holy Spirit and the Virgin
	Mary,
qui sub Pontio Pilato crucifixus	Who was crucified under
est et sepultus,	Pontius Pilate and buried,
tertia die resurrexit a mortuis,	on the third day He rose
	again from the dead,
ascendit in caelos,	He ascended to heaven,
sedet ad dexteram Patris,	He sits at the Father's right
	hand,
unde venturus est iudicare	whence He will come to
vivos et mortuos;	judge living and dead;
Et in Spiritum sanctum,	And in the Holy Spirit,
sanctam ecclesiam, remissionem	the Holy Church, the
peccatorum, carnis	remission of sins, the
resurrectionem.	resurrection of the flesh.

Of these two formularies the second, technically known as the Old Roman Creed (R), is much the more important. In addition to that of Aquileia, a number of other Western creeds have been brought to light and identified.[33] A small minority of them, notably the ones attested by Niceta and St. Augustine, are roughly contemporary with Rufinus, while the great majority, emanating from Italy, North Africa, Spain, and the south of France, belong to somewhat later epochs. All of them, however, including that of Aquileia, have been shown to be lineally descended from the Old Roman Creed. This fact, which is all the more interesting because of the variety of types of Eastern creeds, provides instructive testimony to the extraordinary position occupied by the Roman Church in the early formative centuries. Moreover, the present-day baptismal creed of the West, the formulary which is universally known, to Catholics and Protestants alike, as the Apostles' Creed, is itself simply a provincial elaboration of the Old Roman

Creed. The earliest documentary evidence for this, the Apostles' Creed *par excellence*, occurs in the little treatise *De singulis libris canonicis scarapsus*, [34] which was composed in the second decade of the eighth century by the Benedictine missionary St. Priminius, the founder and first abbot of the famous monastery of Reichenau, near Lake Constance. Its provenance has been the subject of careful scrutiny and keen debate, but the most plausible conclusion is that it was the baptismal creed current in the south-west of France in the seventh century. [35] As a result of the educational and liturgical policy of Charlemagne it found itself enjoying a virtual monopoly in the West, and it was adopted into the baptismal service at Rome itself at some date between the ninth and the eleventh centuries.

If the Old Roman Creed, first explicitly cited by Rufinus, had such an illustrious destiny awaiting it, it could equally look back on a past history of unrivalled antiquity. Rufinus himself was of the opinion that it had undergone no alteration since the age of the Apostles. Even if this was a piously uncritical exaggeration, there is no reason to question his belief in its great age and comparatively conservative character. We have noted that Marcellus of Ancyra was acquainted with a practically identical formulary, in Greek, which in all probability was officially in use at Rome about 340. This Greek text bears no signs of being a translation: consequently scholars have inferred that it represents either the original text of the Roman creed, or at any rate an alternative Greek text designed for Greek-speaking catechumens. On either hypothesis the composition of the formulary must be carried back to the period when the Greek language was still in current use in the Roman Church, that is, at least a hundred years before Marcellus wrote. And this conclusion receives welcome confirmation from the baptismal interrogations which, as we saw above, featured in the baptismal rite recorded by St. Hippolytus. The creed presupposed by this question-naire is not identical with R: the minute differences be-tween the two symbols have supplied a fascinating subject for discussion.[36] But St. Hippolytus's creed is manifestly of the same type as R: more than that, it is related to R in the closest possible way. The time for liturgical fixity and uniformity had not yet arrived, and the two formularies probably existed side by side as variant versions of the Roman baptismal creed.

Thus the Old Roman Creed can be traced back, with its characteristic pattern, phraseology, and contents, at least to the beginning of the third century. Even at that early date it was no artificial improvisation put together to meet the needs of the moment. Rather it was the product of an evolutionary process which, in spite of the fluidity of litur-gical forms in the second century, can still be dimly dis-cerned.[37] The message it conveyed was much more ancient still, being in effect 'the form of doctrine'[38] which the Apostles had proclaimed and which was accepted by the Apostolic Church.

4. RUFINUS AND THE BIBLE

In expounding the creed Rufinus made frequent appeals to Holy Scripture, invariably citing it in the Old Latin version (the *Vetus Latina*). This is the name conventionally given to the Latin translation, or translations (there were a number of different types of text), which the Western Church employed prior to the canonization of St. Jerome's Vulgate. So far as the Old Testament is concerned, the main peculiarity of the Old Latin was its reliance on the

Greek Septuagint rather than on the original Hebrew. Rufinus's preference for the Old Latin need occasion no surprise: a more scientific version was hardly yet in the field. It was only during his residence at Rome, between 382 and 384,[39] that St. Jerome, in response to the request of Pope Damasus, carried through his revision of the existing Latin versions of the New Testament; while the vast enterprise of making an entirely fresh translation of the Old Testament, based on the Hebrew instead of the Greek, occupied him from 391 to 406. Furthermore, like the majority of St. Jerome's contemporaries,[40] Rufinus adopted a distinctly hostile attitude to the project of superseding the traditional Latin texts by something more scholarly. He developed his criticisms at some length in his *Apology against Jerome*,[41] arguing that it was blasphemous to discard the version of Holy Scripture (that is, the Septuagint) which the Apostles themselves had approved, and which St. Peter had presumably delivered to the Roman Church. The fact that St. Paul (he continued), a Hebrew of the Hebrews, had preferred the Septuagint to the Jewish original ought to have served as a deterrent against impious innovation. The only conclusion which heathen observers of this drastic process of emendation could draw was that Christians were not certain in their own minds, and that divine infallibility could not be attributed to their sacred books.

Rufinus's methods of dealing with Scriptural citations were not always consistent. For example, when translating Origen's *Homilies* and *De principiis*, he was content to make his own rendering of any Biblical extracts cited by his author, only having recourse to the Old Latin for particular turns of phrase.[42] On the other hand, when he undertook his translation, or rather abbreviated paraphrase, of

Origen's *Commentary on Romans* a couple or so years after writing the *Commentarius*, he had altered his procedure. The Latin version of the epistle of which he made use has been shown to bear a marked resemblance to that familiar to St. Ambrose and Ambrosiaster, and there can be no doubt that it was the one current in the contemporary Aquileian church.[43] The Scriptural quotations contained in the *Commentarius*, while relatively numerous, are probably too fragmentary and scattered to provide the basis for any equally solid deductions: moreover, he sometimes relied on his memory. It is a reasonable guess, however, and one supported by the intrinsic character of the quotations themselves, that they witness to the version of the Old Latin currently employed in North Italy.

5. THE CANON OF SCRIPTURE

Even more interesting than Rufinus's use of the Old Latin is the account he gives, in chapters 36–38, of the canon of Holy Scripture.[44] Complete agreement had not yet been reached as to the identity and classification of the writings which Christians were expected to regard as inspired and authoritative, and in different ecclesiastical regions different traditions still held sway. That Rufinus was concerned about the problem of the canon is made clear by his attempts to correct what he considered Eusebius's erroneous ideas in his translation of the *Ecclesiastical History*.[45] When he wrote the *Commentarius*, he certainly had before him the canon which St. Cyril of Jerusalem incorporated in the fourth of his *Catechetical Lectures*.[46] He must also have been familiar with the famous canon which St. Athanasius published in his Festal Letter of 367.[47] He had studied in Alexandria, where St.

Athanasius had been bishop, and the latter's influence was probably strong at Aquileia, where he had sojourned during one of his exiles, and where he had founded the monastery in which Rufinus was baptized and received much of his training in the faith. We know also, from certain critical passages of his *Apology*,[48] that he was acquainted with, and strongly disapproved of, St. Jerome's theories about the canon. The views he himself sponsored in the *Commentarius* should not be hastily assumed to represent a purely personal standpoint: it is much more likely that they reflect the dogmatic position of the Aquileian church. This is the point of his emphatic assurances that he was basing himself 'on the records of the Fathers,' and that his list of books conformed to 'the traditional canon handed down to us by the Fathers.'

Rufinus's catalogue divides the books of the Bible into three groups. First, there is the Old Testament, consisting of Genesis, Exodus, Leviticus, Numbers, and Deuteronomy; Josue and Judges, with Ruth; four books of Kings; Paralipomenon, two books of Esdras, and Esther; the four prophets Isaias, Jeremias, Ezechiel, and Daniel, and the single book containing the twelve Minor Prophets; and, finally, Job, the Psalms of David, and three books ascribed to Solomon—Proverbs, Ecclesiastes, and Canticles. In passing he mentions the fact that the four books of Kings are reckoned as two by the Hebrews, and the two books of Esdras as one. Secondly, to the New Testament he assigns, in the following order, the four Gospels, Acts, fourteen Epistles of St. Paul, two Epistles of St. Peter, the Epistle of St. James, the Epistle of St. Jude, three Epistles of St. John, and St. John's Apocalypse. In addition to these he introduces a third category of books which are not strictly canonical, but which he designates 'ecclesiastical.' The characteristic of these is that they may be freely read in the churches, but may not be invoked as authoritative for doctrine. As appendages to the Old Testament he enumerates Wisdom of Solomon, Wisdom of Sirach (otherwise called Ecclesiasticus), Tobias, Judith, and the books of Machabees; as appendages to the New Testament, The Shepherd of Hermas, The Two Ways, and The Judgment of Peter.

For a proper appreciation of the importance of this catalogue we should need to study it in the context of the history of the canon generally. Here we have only space to underline a few of its most significant features. In the first place, we notice that, while Rufinus (in conformity with the practice of the early Fathers) limited the Old Testament proper to the books of the Hebrew canon, he seems to have discarded the traditional notion that it contained twenty-two books corresponding to the number of letters in the Hebrew alphabet. Both St. Athanasius and St. Jerome, as well as Rufinus's master Origen, stressed the number twenty-two, and accepted the parallelism between the books of Holy Scripture and the letters of the alphabet.[49] In the second place, Rufinus's order differs from those of St. Cyril, St. Athanasius, and St. Jerome. According to his arrangement, the historical books are classed together (this point he probably derived from St. Cyril), then come the major and the minor prophets, and the collection is rounded off with the poetical books (to adopt the description given by St. Cyril). Both St. Cyril and St. Athanasius placed the poetical books between the historical and the prophetical, and both again placed the single book of the Lesser Prophets before the Great Prophets. St. Athanasius, moreover, omitted Esther from his canonical list, and both he and St. Cyril attached Baruch, Lamentations, and the Epistle of Jeremias to Jeremias. Rufinus, however, does not mention these. On the other hand, St. Jerome characteristically adhered to the Hebrew arrangement, dividing the Old Testament into the Law, the Prophets, and the Writings (Hagiographa), and reckoning Paralipomenon, Esdras, and Esther among the last mentioned.

As regards the New Testament, Rufinus's catalogue discloses that all the twenty-seven canonical books were recognized as such at Aquileia about A.D. 400. Furthermore, with the exception of the Catholic Epistles, the order later to be universally adopted under the influence of the Vulgate was apparently already established. As regards the first of these points, Rufinus's implied acceptance of the Pauline authorship of Hebrews deserves note. The hesitations of the West on this score are well known, and even writers like Ambrosiaster [50] preferred to regard it as anonymous. The Synod of Carthage (397) reflected these doubts, classifying Hebrews separately from the thirteen admitted epistles,[51] and St. Augustine himself seems to have wavered in his attitude, accepting it as Pauline in his earlier period, but in his old age treating it as anonymous.[52] Rufinus was also ahead of many in his arrangement of the books. Both St. Cyril and St. Athanasius had placed the Catholic Epistles immediately after Acts and before the Paulines, while in Pope Innocent's famous letter to Exsuperius of Toulouse, Acts stood at the end just before the Apocalypse.[53] The order in which Rufinus chose to group the Catholic Epistles is unprecedented. To some [54] it has suggested either that he wanted to bring St. Peter into close proximity with St. Paul, or that he considered that St. Peter's position as prince of the Apostles merited special recognition. Finally, his stress on the fact that St. Peter and

St. James were Apostles may be an indication of his theory that canonicity depended on apostolic authorship.

Rufinus's designation of a class of 'ecclesiastical' books is of particular interest and importance. The basis of the distinction he sought to establish lay partly in the difference between the Hebrew and the so-called Alexandrian canons of the Old Testament, and partly in the existence of a number of Christian writings which hovered on the fringe of the New Testament. For centuries the attitude of the Church towards the additional books comprised in the Alexandrian, or Greek, canon lacked precise definition. Its ultimate decision was to range the majority of these (the deutero-canonical writings) alongside the twenty-two books traditionally acknowledged by Palestinian Judaism as inspired Scripture. On the other hand, it firmly restricted the New Testament to the twenty-seven apostolic books now comprised in it, rejecting the handful of apocryphal works which had sometimes seemed claimants to a place in the canon.

In the fourth century a great variety of opinion existed as to the status of both these groups. If the West as a whole was prepared to accept the deutero-canonical books of the Old Testament, the East and such Western theologians as maintained close contact with the East were still disturbed by grave doubts. Rufinus's distinction, and the grounds on which he based it, recall the directions laid down by St. Athanasius in his famous Festal Letter.[55] After enumerating the canonical books and declaring that 'in these alone the good news of the teaching of true religion is proclaimed,' he went on to state that there were certain other books which, while not canonical, had been 'authorized by the Fathers to be read by those who are just coming forward to receive oral instruction in the word of true religion.'

These books, he added, were Wisdom, Wisdom of Sirach, Esther, Judith, Tobias, the Didache of the Apostles, and The Shepherd. He was the first Eastern writer to adopt this line, and Rufinus was the first to make a similar distinction in the West. But we should notice that, whereas at Alexandria the deutero-canonical books were to be studied only by catechumens, at Aquileia they were apparently read in church along with the canonical books proper. The only difference was that the 'ecclesiastical' writings were books of edification, and could not be appealed to in support of doctrine. But if Rufinus's attitude marked a slight advance on that of St. Athanasius, it differed radically from that of St. Cyril and St. Jerome. The former insisted[56] that only the twenty-two books of the Old Testament and the canonical list of the New should be read: 'let all the rest be put aside in a secondary grade. Whatever books are not read in church, these read not even by thyself.' It is noteworthy that, in spite of this severity, he did not hesitate, in his own works, to quote the deutero-canonical books.[57] The attitude of St. Jerome was even more downright. Occasionally, it is true, he seemed to approximate to Rufinus's position, declaring in one passage that Tobias, Judith, and Machabees 'are not among the canonical Scriptures,' but that 'the Church reads them for the edification of the people, and not for the support of ecclesiastical doctrine.'[58] His true and characteristic position, however, is revealed in his *Prologus galeatus*, where he affirms that the Old Testament must be confined to the books of the Jewish canon, and that anything not found in the Hebrew must be dismissed as apocryphal.[59]

Rufinus's discussion of the canon has sometimes been said to betray the influence of St. Athanasius's teaching in his Festal Letter.[60] Yet it should be clear that, while in harmony with the great bishop of Alexandria on a number of points, he was in other respects independent of him and took a line of his own. After all, he was 'one of the greatest Christian travellers of his age,' and was thus exposed to influences from several quarters. It would be a mistake, however, to interpret his remarks as necessarily reflecting either purely personal predilections or the impact of traditions he had met with in the course of his extensive journeys. The language he employs, as well as the catechetical intent of his little treatise, supports the view that the canon of which he supplies a glimpse was in all probability the one currently accepted in the Aquileian church. As such it merits closer attention than has sometimes been bestowed upon it.

6. BIBLIOGRAPHICAL NOTE

The translation which follows has been based on the Latin text of D. Vallarsi, published at Verona in 1742 and reprinted by J. P. Migne in vol. 21 of his *Patrologia Latina*, cols. 335–86. The text of Baluze (see his *Cypriani Opera* [Paris 1726]) is at many points more reliable, but Vallarsi's has been chosen in view of its more general accessibility. The most useful annotations are still those printed in Migne. E. F. Morison published a handy edition of the Latin text, with introduction and brief notes in English, and also a second volume containing an English translation, in 1916 (London). Reference may also be made to the translation, prolegomena, and short notes published by W. H. Fremantle in the third volume of the 'Nicene and Post-Nicene Fathers' series (Oxford and New York 1892).

The most exhaustive and scholarly study of Rufinus

available is F. X. Murphy's *Rufinus of Aquileia, His Life and Works* (Washington 1945). The student should also consult the article 'Rufin d'Aquilée' by G. Bardy in *Dictionnaire de théologie catholique*, vol. 14, as well as M. Villain's articles 'Rufin d'Aquilée, l'étudiant et le moine,' in *Nouvelle revue théologique* 64 (1937) 5–33; 139–61.

Important discussions of Rufinus's witness to the baptismal creeds of Rome and Aquileia will be found in F. Kattenbusch, *Das apostolische Symbol*, 2 vols. (Leipzig 1894–1900), and in J. N. D. Kelly, *Early Christian Creeds* (London 1950), esp. chapters 4 and 6. For Rufinus's treatment of the Scriptural canon, see M. Stenzel's valuable article in *Biblica* 23 (1942) 43–61.

A COMMENTARY ON
THE APOSTLES' CREED BY
TYRANNIUS RUFINUS, OF AQUILEIA,
PRIEST

INTRODUCTION

1. I have little inclination, and as little capacity, faithful Bishop Lawrence,[1] for writing: I am aware of the danger of exposing my slender talents to the world's criticism. In your letter, however, you are so rash (please forgive the word) as to charge me in the name of Christ's sacraments, which I hold in the profoundest reverence, to write you an essay on the faith based on the contents and pattern of the Creed. Admittedly the burden you impose exceeds my powers: I cannot forget the acute maxim of sensible men, 'Speaking even the truth about God has its perils.' Still, provided you pray for me, thereby making the fulfilment of your request easier, I shall try to produce something, though more for the sake of complying with your wishes than out of any presumption on my part.[2] I only hope it may be deemed worthy, I shall not say to exercise the minds of advanced Christians, but to be adapted to the hearing of little ones in Christ and mere novices.[3]

It has come to my notice that quite a few eminent writers[4] have published concise and doctrinally sound manuals on the subject. But I know too that the heretic Photinus,[5] instead of explaining the sense of the clauses to his audience, made it his object to twist straightforward orthodox statements so as to bolster up his own ideas. And this despite the fact that the Holy Spirit has taken care that the text should contain nothing ambiguous, obscure, or inconsistent. In fact, our creed may be regarded as accurately fulfilling the prophecy: *Summing up His word and cutting it short in justice: because a short word will the Lord make upon the earth.*[6] My endeavour, therefore, will be to restore and emphasize the plain, simple meaning of the Apostles' words, and at the same time to fill in the gaps left by my predecessors. But to make the drift of this *short word*, as I have called it, clearer, I shall trace back to their origin the circumstances which led to this traditional formula being entrusted to the churches.

APOSTOLIC COMPOSITION OF THE CREED

2. After our Lord's ascension (so runs the tradition of our forefathers), with the coming of the Holy Spirit tongues of fire settled on the Apostles individually. They were thus enabled to speak a variety of different languages, with the result that they found no nation strange to them, and no foreign speech beyond their powers of comprehension. The Lord then commanded them to journey separately to different countries to preach the word of God. When they were on the point of taking leave of each other, they first settled on a common form for their future preaching, so that they might not find themselves, widely dispersed as they would be, delivering divergent messages to the people they were persuading to believe in Christ. So they all assembled in one spot and, being filled with the Holy Spirit, drafted this short summary, as I have explained, of their future preaching, each contributing the

clause he judged fitting: and they decreed that it should be
handed out as standard teaching to converts.[7]

The name they decided to give it, for a number of excellent reasons, was *symbol*.[8] *Symbol* in Greek can mean both
'token' and 'collection,' that is, a joint whole to which
several persons contribute. This is what the Apostles did in
the case of our formulary, each contributing the clause
he judged fitting. At the same time, it gets the name
'token' or 'watchword' from the fact that in those days,
as the Apostle Paul vouches and as is testified in Acts,[9]
numerous vagabond Jews posing as apostles of Christ were
going about preaching, their motive being the desire for
gain, or gluttony. They used the name of Christ, but their
message did not conform to the traditional outline. The
Apostles therefore prescribed the creed as a badge for distinguishing the man who preached the truth about Christ
in harmony with their rule. In civil wars, it is said, a
parallel practice is observed. There the pattern of weapons
is similar, the language of both sides is identical, their behaviour and methods of fighting are the same; and so, to
exclude the possibility of treachery, both generals furnish
their men with recognizable passwords, called in Latin
signa or *indicia*. Then, if someone of doubtful identity turns
up, he can be asked for his password, and will be revealed
as friend or foe. Furthermore, the story continues, the
reason why the creed is not written down on paper or
parchment, but is retained in the believers' hearts, is to
ensure that it has been learned from the tradition handed
down from the Apostles, and not from written texts,
which occasionally fall into the hands of unbelievers.[10]

To repeat, when they were on the point of setting out on
their preaching mission, the Apostles established this token
of their common agreement in the faith. They did not

behave like Noe's sons, who, when taking leave of one another, built a tower of baked bricks and tar with its summit aimed at the sky.[11] Rather they constructed, out of living stones and pearls supplied by the Lord, a monument of faith to stand firm in the face of adversaries. They did not want the winds to buffet it, or the floods to undermine it, or the violence of storms and tempests to shake it. As a punishment well deserved, since on the eve of their separation they built a tower of pride, Noe's sons were afflicted with confusion of languages, so that none of them could understand his neighbour's speech. But the Apostles, erecting a tower of faith, were rewarded with the knowledge of, and the ability to use, all languages. In the one case you had the proof of sin, in the other, of faith.

APOSTOLIC CHARACTER OF THE ROMAN CREED

3. But it is now time for me to comment on these pearls themselves. Right in the forefront is set the fountainhead and source of them all, in the statement: I BELIEVE IN GOD THE FATHER ALMIGHTY.[12] But before I start discussing the implication of the words, I think it appropriate to mention that certain additions are to be found in this article in some churches. No such development, however, can be detected in the case of the church of the city of Rome.[13] The reason, I suppose, is that no heresy has ever originated there. Also, the ancient custom is maintained there whereby candidates who are on the point of receiving the grace of baptism deliver the creed publicly, in the hearing of the congregation of the faithful.[14] As a result, since those who have preceded them in the faith are listening attentively, the interpolation of even

a single article is not tolerated. Elsewhere, to the best of
my understanding, the presence of heretics seems to have
occasioned the insertion of clauses, the idea being that they
would help to exclude novelties of doctrine.[15] For my part,
I propose to base myself on the text to which I pledged
myself when I was baptized[16] in the church of Aquileia.

THE NECESSITY OF BELIEF

Well then, I BELIEVE stands right in the foreground,
as the Apostle Paul insists when writing to the Hebrews:
*For he that cometh to God must first of all believe that He is,
and is a rewarder to them that believe in Him.*[17] The prophet,
too, points out: *If you will not believe, you will not understand.*[18] Since you want the door of understanding opened
to you, it is only right that you should first of all confess
that you believe.[19] No one, for example, embarks on the
sea, committing his life to the watery depths, without first
believing in the possibility of his survival. No farmer
buries his seeds under the upturned sods or scatters his
fruits on the earth without the confident belief that,
fostered by the rains and the co-operation of the sun's
warmth, the soil will multiply the fruit and bear its crop,
ripening it with favourable winds. In fact, there is nothing
in life than can be transacted without a preliminary readiness to believe. Is it then at all surprising that, when we
approach God, we first of all confess that we believe, seeing
that without belief even the common routine of life cannot be accomplished? I have set these axioms down at the
outset because pagans are in the habit of objecting that
our religion lacks a rational basis, depending solely on the
persuasion of belief.[20] Consequently I have demonstrated
that, unless belief exercises its prior influence, nothing can

be done, or, for that matter, stay as it was. Marriages, I may add, are contracted in the belief that a family will result. Children are sent to school to study in the belief that the schoolmasters' instruction will settle into their pupils' minds. A monarch assumes the emblems of sovereignty in the belief that peoples, cities, the armed forces themselves, will obey him. But if no one undertakes enterprises like these without first believing that certain results will ensue, is it not all the more understandable that belief should be the way to the knowledge of God?

THE BEING AND FATHERHOOD OF GOD

4. But let us notice what this brief article of the creed puts before us next. I BELIEVE, it states, IN GOD THE FATHER ALMIGHTY. Almost without exception the Eastern churches give this in the form, [21] I BELIEVE IN *ONE* GOD THE FATHER ALMIGHTY. Again, in the following article, where we say, AND IN CHRIST JESUS, HIS ONLY SON, OUR LORD, they read,[22] AND IN OUR ONE LORD, JESUS CHRIST, HIS ONLY SON. They confess, you see, ONE GOD and ONE LORD, in deference to the Apostle Paul.[23] But I shall come back to this in what follows. In the meantime let us examine what is meant by, IN GOD THE FATHER ALMIGHTY.

'God,' so far as human intelligence can conceive, is the designation of the absolutely supreme nature or substance. 'Father' is a term pointing to a secret, inexpressible mystery. When 'God' is uttered, you are to understand a substance without beginning or end, simple, uncompounded, invisible, incorporeal, ineffable, incomprehensible: a substance in which there is nothing accidental, nothing creaturely. For He who is the originator of all things is Himself without origin. When 'Father' is uttered, you are to understand the Father of the Son, the Son being the image of the above-mentioned substance. Just as no one is called 'master' without having some property or some servant to exercise mastery over, and just as no one is called 'teacher' unless he has a pupil, so it is impossible for anyone to be called 'Father' unless he has a son. Thus the very title by which God is called 'Father' proves that a Son coexists side by side with the Father.[24]

I would rather, however, you did not discuss how God the Father generated the Son, and did not plunge too inquisitively into the depths of the mystery.[25] There is a danger that, in prying too persistently into the brightness of inaccessible light, you may find yourself deprived of the tiny glimpse which is all the good God vouchsafes to mortals. Alternatively, if you judge this a subject which justifies every sort of scrutiny, first employ your mind on things which concern ourselves. If you have the skill to unravel them satisfactorily, speed on then from terrestrial things to things heavenly, and from visible to invisible. First of all explain, if you can, how the mind within you generates its word, and what the spirit of memory in your mind is.[26] Explain how these, for all their diversity in reality and operation, form a unity in substance or nature, and how, while proceeding from the mind, they are never separated from it. If, in spite of their being within our very selves and of the substance of our souls, these facts remain mysterious to us because of their invisibility to bodily sight, let us turn our attention to things more open to view. How, for example, does a river-source generate the river from itself? By what hidden force is it

carried on to form a flowing stream? How is it that, while
the river and its source are one and indivisible, the river
cannot be taken for or described as the source, nor con-
versely, and yet anyone who sees the river sees the source
also? First practise yourself in clearing up puzzles like
these, and discuss to the best of your ability things within
your grasp: then you can climb to loftier themes. Do not
imagine that I would urge you to ascend all at once from
earth to heaven: allow me first to escort you to the firmament we can see with our physical eyes. Investigate there,
if you are able, the nature of the visible light, discussing
how this blaze in the heavens generates glittering light
from itself, at the same time producing heat, and how these
form three realities yet one single substance. Even if you
can explain each of these mysteries, you must realize that
the mystery of divine generation is different from and
loftier than they in proportion as the Creator is more
powerful than His creatures, the Artificer more excellent
than His works, and He who eternally exists nobler than
one who has come into existence out of nothing.

We must believe, then, without argument, that God is
Father of His only-begotten Son, our Lord. Indeed, it is
blasphemous for the servant to argue about his Master's
nativity. The Father has borne witness from heaven,
saying: *This is my beloved Son, in whom I am well pleased:
hear Him.*[27] The Father says He is His Son, and bids us
hear Him. The Son says: *He that seeth me seeth the Father
also*, and: *I and the Father are one*, and: *I came forth from God,
and came into this world.*[28] Is anyone entitled to thrust himself argumentatively between these statements of the
Father and the Son, dividing the Godhead, cleaving
asunder Its volition, disrupting the substance, cutting what
is spirit into parts, denying the truth of what the Truth

affirms? God is therefore truly the Father, inasmuch as He is Father of truth; He does not create the Son from outside Himself, but generates Him from His own substance. That is to say, being wise, He generates Wisdom, being just, Justice, being eternal, the Eternal, being immortal, the Immortal, being invisible, the Invisible. Because He is light, He generates brightness, and because He is mind, the Word.

GOD'S UNITY AND OMNIPOTENCE

5. As for my statement that the Eastern churches teach the existence of ONE GOD THE FATHER ALMIGHTY and ONE LORD, we should take this as implying that God is absolutely, and not just numerically, one.[29] To give an illustration, 'one' is used numerically when we refer to one man or one horse, for a second or third man or horse is conceivable. But when 'one' is used without any possibility of a second or third being added, the word then has an absolute, not a numerical, significance. For example, when we speak of the sun as one, the usage of the word implies that a second or third cannot be added: there is, you see, only one sun. Much more so in the case of God, when we describe Him as one, do we use the term in an absolute, not a numerical, sense. That is to say, He is described as one because there is no second God. In the case of our Lord, too, our interpretation must be similar, namely, that there is only one Lord Jesus Christ through whom God the Father exercises His universal sway.

That is why the clause which follows defines Him as almighty. ALMIGHTY is applied to Him on account of the dominion He has over the universe.[30] But the Father governs the universe through the Son, as the Apostle himself states: *For through Him were all things created, visible and invisible, whether thrones, or dominations, or principalities, or powers.*[31] Again, writing to the Hebrews, he states: *Because through Him He made the world, and appointed Him heir of all things.*[32] By 'appointed' we are to take him as meaning 'generated.' But if the Father made the world through Him, and if through Him all things were created and He is the heir of all things, it must be through Him that He wields His sway over the universe. Just as light is generated from light, and truth from truth, so Almighty is generated from Almighty. So we read in John's Apocalypse about the Seraphim: *And they rested not day and night, saying, Holy, Holy, Holy, Lord God of Sabaoth, who was, and who is, and is to come, the Almighty.*[33] He then who is to come is called Almighty; and who else is to come save Christ, the Son of God?

To the foregoing are added INVISIBLE and IMPASSIBLE. These two predicates, we should notice, are absent from the creed of the Roman church. They were interpolated [34] amongst us, as is well known, to meet the heresy of Sabellius, which our people call Patripassianism.[35] This is the heresy which alleges that the Father Himself was born from the Virgin, and declares that He was thereby made visible and suffered in the flesh. In order to eliminate any such impious notions about the Father, our predecessors appear to have added these predicates, describing Him as INVISIBLE and IMPASSIBLE. For obviously, it was the Son, not the Father, who became incarnate and was born from human flesh, and the Son who through this birth in human flesh was made visible and passible. So far as concerns the immortal substance of the Godhead, which the Son shares equally and identically with the Father, neither the Father nor the Son nor the Holy Spirit, according to our faith, is visible or passible. Only in so far as He stooped to assume human flesh did the Son make Himself visible or did He suffer in the flesh. The prophet himself foretold this in these words: *This is our God: there shall no other be accounted of in comparison of Him. He found out all the way of instruction, and gave it to Jacob His servant and to Israel His beloved. Afterwards He was seen upon the earth, and conversed with men.*[36]

CHRIST'S NAMES AND DIVINE SONSHIP

6. The next article runs thus: AND IN CHRIST JESUS, HIS ONLY SON, OUR LORD. 'Jesus' is a Hebrew word[38] which we translate 'Saviour.' His title 'Christ' is derived from 'chrism,' that is, anointing.[39] As regards the former, we read in the books of Moses that, when Osee the son of Nun was appointed leader of the people, he had his name changed from Osee to Jesus.[40] The idea was to emphasize that this was an appropriate name for princes and leaders with whom lay the responsibility for *saving* the people attached to them. So both were called Jesus—both he who, when the people had been brought up out of Egypt and released from their wanderings in the desert, guided them into the promised land; and He who brought His people up out of the darkness of ignorance and, recalling them from the distractions of the world, guided them to the kingdom of heaven. As regards 'Christ,' it is a title proper either to high priests or to kings. In former times both high priests and kings were consecrated with the oil of chrism.[41] But whereas they, as was fitting for corruptible mortals, were anointed with material, corruptible oils, our Lord was installed as Christ

by the anointing of the Holy Spirit. So the Bible describes Him as, *Whom the Father anointed with the Holy Spirit sent from heaven.*[42] Isaias, too, speaking in the person of the Son, foretold this figuratively in the words: *The Spirit of the Lord is upon me: because He hath anointed me, He hath sent me to preach the gospel to the poor.*[43]

We have explained, then, the meaning of 'Jesus' (the Saviour of His people), and of 'Christ' (one appointed high priest for ever).[44] In what follows we can catch a glimpse of the Subject of these titles. HIS ONLY SON, the Creed proceeds, OUR LORD. Here its teaching is that Jesus, of whom we have spoken, and Christ, on whose title we have commented, is the only Son of God, and our Lord. The object of adding that He is the only Son of God, our Lord, is to prevent you from supposing an earthly significance to be contained in the preceding description. He is the unique offspring of a unique Father, just as there is only one brightness of light and only one word of the understanding. Being incorporeal, His generation neither results in plurality nor involves division: He who is born is not separated from His begetter.[45] He is unique, as thought is to the mind, as its word to the understanding, as his courage to the hero, as wisdom to the wise man. Just as the Apostle calls the Father *the only wise*, so the Son alone is designated Wisdom.[46] The Son is therefore unique. And although He is identical with the Father in glory, eternity, virtue, royalty, and power, He does not possess these unoriginately, as the Father does, but by derivation from the Father, as a Son, though a Son without beginning and equal to His Father. Also, while He is Himself head of all things, the Father is head of Him, for Scripture says: *Because God is the head of Christ.*[47]

7. When you hear the word SON, the conception you

form should not be of human birth in the flesh:[48] you should remember that the term is being used of an incorporeal substance, simple and uncompounded. As I have already pointed out above, there is nothing material in the way the understanding generates its word or the mind its thought, any more than in the way light produces brightness from itself: in such acts of generation we do not imply any imperfection. But if so, how much purer and more reverent ought our conclusions about the Creator of all these things to be?

You may, however, object: 'The kind of generation you quote as a parallel is insubstantial. The brightness which light produces is not a substance, nor is the word which the understanding begets a substance. But the Son of God, it is claimed, is begotten as a substance.'[49] In reply I would argue first of all as follows. Even in other fields, when illustrations are advanced, the resemblance they provide to the object they are supposed to illustrate cannot possibly hold good in every respect: the resemblance holds good only for that one aspect which they are chosen to illustrate.[50] For example, when we read in the Gospel: *The kingdom of heaven is like to leaven, which a woman hid in three measures of meal*,[51] we are surely not to infer that the kingdom of heaven is like leaven in all respects, its substance being capable of being handled and perishable, and so being liable to become sour and to decay. The sole point of the illustration would seem to be to demonstrate how, as a result of such an insignificant thing as the preaching of God's word, men's minds can be bound together in unity by the leaven of faith. Similarly, when we read: *The kingdom of heaven is like to a net cast into the sea, which draws in every kind of fish*,[52] we are surely not to infer that the reality of the kingdom of heaven is comparable in every respect with the twine out of which we construct a net and the knots by which the meshes are fastened together. The sole point of this analogy would seem to be to show how, just as a net hauls fishes to the shore from the depths of the sea, so human souls are delivered from the abysmal errors of this world by the gospel of the kingdom of heaven. All this makes it clear that illustrations do not resemble the objects they illustrate in every particular. Otherwise, if they were similar in all respects, they would not be termed illustrations, but would obviously be the very things under discussion.

8. In the second place, we must point out that it is impossible for any creature to be such as its Creator. Just as there is no exact illustration of divine substance, so there is no exact illustration of Deity. In addition, I would remind you that every creature is derived from nothingness. Consequently, if the spark which is so insubstantial and yet is fire generates from itself a creature made out of nothingness, thereby preserving its original status, why should it be inconceivable for the substance of that eternal Light, which has always existed because it contains nothing insubstantial in Itself, to produce from Itself a Brightness which is substantial? Hence the correctness of the Son's being described as ONLY:[53] because He was born in this way, He is unique and alone. Nothing that is unique can admit of any comparison: no more can He who is the maker of all things bear any likeness in substance to the things He has made. This then is Christ Jesus, the only Son of God, who is also our Lord. 'Only' can be applied to Him both as Son and as Lord. For Jesus Christ is 'only' both as God's authentic Son and as our sole Lord.[54] All other sons of God, though designated sons, have that title by the grace of adoption, not as a result of any natural

relationship.[55] If others bear the title Lord, they have it by virtue of an authority bestowed, not inherent. He alone is God's only Son, He alone our only Lord, as the Apostle himself implies: *And one Lord Jesus Christ, by whom are all things.*[56]

THE VIRGIN BIRTH

9. So, after setting out the inexpressible mystery of the Son's generation from the Father, our authorized summary of the faith proceeds now to the dispensation by which He humbled Himself for man's salvation. Above it described Him as God's 'only Son' and as 'our Lord': now it speaks of Him as WHO WAS BORN BY THE HOLY SPIRIT FROM THE VIRGIN MARY.[57] This birth among men concerns the historical revelation; the other has to do with the divine substance. If this one expresses condescension, the other involves God's nature. He is born by the Holy Spirit from the Virgin. For this passage chaster ears and a purer mind are called for. What you are expected to understand here is that He who, as you have already learned, was born ineffably from the Father had a shrine constructed for Him by the Holy Spirit in the recesses of the Virgin's womb. And just as no imperfection is conceivable in the sanctification bestowed by the Holy Spirit, so we should not envisage any defilement in the birth from the Virgin. In this birth the world had something unprecedented vouchsafed it, and for a very good reason. For it is congruous that He who is only Son in heaven should be only Son on earth as well, and therefore should be born in a unique manner.

The predictions of the prophets about Him, to the effect that *A virgin shall conceive, and bear a son,*[58] are familiar to everybody, and are repeatedly quoted in the Gospels. But

the miraculous manner of the birth itself was long ago
anticipated by the prophet Ezechiel: in a figure [59] he called
Mary 'the gate of the Lord,' meaning that through her the
Lord entered the world. Thus he says: *But the gate which
looks towards the East shall be shut, and shall not be opened, and
no one shall pass through it; for the Lord God of Israel shall
pass through it, and it shall be shut.* [60] Could a more explicit
hint have been given of the Virgin's being kept inviolate?
The gate which was shut was her virginity. Through it the
Lord God of Israel entered; through it He advanced into
this world from the Virgin's womb. And, because her virginity was preserved intact, the Virgin's gate has remained
shut for ever. [61] The Holy Spirit is therefore mentioned as
the creator both of the Lord's flesh and of His shrine.

10. At this point you should also begin to appreciate the
Holy Spirit's majesty. The Gospel narrative itself testifies
to Him, reporting that, when the angel spoke to the Virgin
and said: *Thou shalt bring forth a son, and thou shalt call
His name Jesus. For He shall save His people from their sins,* [62]
she replied: *How shall this be done, because I know not
man?* The angel answered her: *The Holy Spirit shall come
upon thee, and the Power of the Most High shall overshadow
thee. Therefore the Holy which shall be born of thee shall be
called the Son of God.* [63] You observe, then, the Trinity
operating in unison. The Holy Spirit, it is said, comes upon
the Virgin, and the Power of the Most High overshadows
her. But what is the Power of the Most High, if not
Christ Himself, who is the power of God and the wisdom
of God? [64] And to whom does this Power belong? To the
Most High, says Scripture. So we have here the Most
High, the Power of the Most High, and the Holy Spirit.
So we have here the Trinity, which is everwhere concealed
and yet is everywhere manifested, which is distinct in

names and persons, but is inseparable in the substance of Godhead. Although only the Son is born from the Virgin, the Most High is nevertheless present, and the Holy Spirit also is present to sanctify both the conception and the bringing forth of the Virgin.

11. Arguments like these, based as they are on the Bible prophecies, may perhaps silence Jews, despite their incredulous refusal to believe. But pagans are in the habit of laughing at us when they hear us preaching a virgin birth.[65] A brief reply to their calumnies is therefore called for. Every birth, I take it, depends on three conditions: there must be a woman of ripe years, she must have intercourse with a man, and there must be no impediment of barrenness blocking her womb. One of these three conditions, the presence of a man, was wanting in the birth we Christians proclaim. Our assertion is that, since the offspring born was not an earthly but a heavenly man, this function was fulfilled by the heavenly Spirit, the Virgin's purity remaining inviolate.

Yet why should conception by a virgin be deemed astonishing, seeing that, as is well known, the Eastern bird called phoenix is either born or reborn without a mate, continually remaining one and continually replacing itself by birth or rebirth?[66] As for bees, it is notorious that they are ignorant of any mating, and do not produce their young by ordinary travail.[67] There are other creatures, too, which are found to be subject to a similar law of birth. Are we then to think it incredible that divine power, with the restoration of the whole world as its object, should accomplish something for which precedents can be found even in the generation of animals? It amazes me that Gentiles should regard this as impossible, believing as they do that Minerva was born from Jupiter's brain.[68] Yet what could put a greater strain on belief, or be more contrary to nature? In the case we are discussing there is a woman, the natural order is adhered to, conception takes place, and the offspring is born after the appropriate interval. But in the latter case no female is involved: all we have is the male and an act of birth. Why should anyone who accepts this feel qualms about our teaching? They also allege that Father Bacchus was produced from Jupiter's thigh:[69] another species of marvel, yet one which they find credible. Venus, too, whom they call Aphrodite, they believe to have been generated from foam of the sea, as her compound name suggests;[70] while Castor and Pollux, they declare, were born from an egg,[71] and the Myrmidons from ants.[72] There are countless other stories which, for all their contravention of the natural order, they nevertheless devoutly believe, as about the stones scattered by Deucalion and Pyrrha from which a crop of men sprang up.[73] Yet, while accepting all these fictions, and others too, the one miracle which strikes them as impossible is that a young woman should conceive a divine offspring, not by defiling contact with a man, but by the inspiration of God. If belief comes to them so hardly, they should never have given credence to so many disgusting extravagances. On the other hand, if they find belief easy, they ought to have accepted these honourable, pious articles of ours much more readily than those discreditable, debasing legends.

12. Perhaps, however, their contention is that, granted the possibility with God of a virgin's conceiving, the possibility of her bearing a child must be admitted, but they find something unworthy in One so majestic having to traverse a woman's womb. Even if there was no defilement resulting from intercourse with a male, there was the unseemly and degrading manipulation incidental to the

delivery itself.[74] Let us pause for a moment to meet their objection at their own level. If someone should see a child being suffocated in a deep quagmire, and, himself a full-grown, powerful man, should plunge into the mire at its extreme edge, if I may so put it, in order to rescue the dying child, would you upbraid him for dirtying himself by treading on an insignificant quantity of mud, or would you rather commend him for so compassionately bestowing life on someone at the point of death? But this argument might be pressed in the case of an ordinary man. Let us return to the nature of Him who was born. How much inferior to Him do you suppose the nature of the sun to be? Precisely to the degree, no doubt, to which creatures are inferior to their Creator. Ask yourself, then, if a ray of sunlight settles on a muddy pool, whether it receives from it any taint of pollution.[75] Or does the sun sustain any loss through shedding its light on disgusting objects? Or take fire: its nature is much humbler than the things we have been discussing. Yet no one believes fire to be polluted through having foul or repulsive matter thrust on to it. If there is general agreement about this in the case of material things, do you really imagine that any pollution or defilement can result in the case of the supreme, incorporeal nature which transcends fire and light? But there is a further point which you should notice. Our teaching is that man was created by God out of the clay of the earth. But if God is reckoned to suffer defilement when restoring His work, much more must we suppose Him to have suffered when creating it in the first instance. Furthermore, it is a waste of time inquiring why He traversed anything 'immodest,' seeing that you cannot explain why He created such. Indeed, it is not nature, but current convention, that has taught us to see immodesty here. Actually, all the parts of the body have been fashioned out of the selfsame clay, being distinguished from one another by their uses and their natural functions.

13. There is, however, a further consideration we ought not to overlook in the solution of this problem: God's substance, being absolutely incorporeal, cannot in the first instance be introduced into bodies, or contained by them, without the mediation of some spiritual substance capable of receiving the divine Spirit. To give a parallel, we may say that light is able to illuminate all the parts of the body: nevertheless, it cannot be received by any of them save the eye alone, only the eye being receptive of light. Similarly, when the Son of God was born from the Virgin, He was not in the first instance associated with the flesh alone, but was begotten with a soul mediating between the flesh and the Deity.[76] Thus, with the soul acting as medium and containing the Word of God in the secret citadel of rational spirit, God was born from the Virgin without any of that loss of majesty which you suspect. It is wrong, therefore, to find anything degrading in a transaction in which the sanctifying power of the Spirit was present, and in which the soul, capable as it was of receiving the Godhead, formed a link between It and the flesh. You should not presuppose anything impossible in a transaction in which the Power of the Most High was at work, nor should you draw analogies from the weakness of human nature when the fullness of Deity was present.

THE SIGNIFICANCE OF THE CRUCIFIXION

14. CRUCIFIED UNDER PONTIUS PILATE, AND BURIED, HE DESCENDED TO HELL.[77] The

Apostle Paul teaches that we ought to have *the eyes of our heart enlightened*, that we may understand *what is the height and breadth and depth.*[78] These words, *the height and breadth and depth*, are a description of the cross. The portion of it which was fixed in the earth he called *depth.* By *height* he meant the part which stretches above the earth and towers upwards, by *breadth* the parts which extend outwards to the right hand and to the left. But seeing there are so many modes of death by which men may depart this life, why should the Apostle want us to have our hearts enlightened and to appreciate the reason for the choice of crucifixion, out of all the modes which were possible, for the Saviour's death? Surely the inference we should draw is that His cross was a triumph; it was a trophy of distinction.[79] A triumph, however, is the token of the defeat of an enemy. At His coming, then, as the Apostle says, Christ reduced three kingdoms simultaneously to subjection (he brings this out in the words: *For in the name of Jesus every knee shall bow, of those that are in heaven, on earth, and under the earth*),[80] and in His death He vanquished all three. Consequently a form of death was devised which symbolized this mystery. He was to be raised aloft in the air, thereby conquering the powers of the air and gaining a victory over the heavenly rulers on high.[81] His outstretched hands, moreover, according to the inspired prophet,[82] He held out all day long to the people who were on the earth, testifying to the unbelievers and welcoming believers; while with the portion of the cross buried in the earth He brought the underworld into subjection to Himself.

15. For in the beginning (if I may touch briefly on matters hid from the uninitiated), when God created the world, He appointed and set over it certain heavenly powers to exercise authority and government over the

·human race. Moses makes this plain in his Canticle in Deuteronomy, saying: *When the Lofty One divided the nations, . . . He appointed the bounds of the nations according to the number of God's angels.*[83] Several of these, however, including the one called the Prince of the World,[84] refused to administer the power entrusted them by God in harmony with the terms on which they had received it. Instead, they instructed mankind to obey, not God's ordinances, but their own criminal suggestions. As a result, the bonds of sin were written out against us: as the Prophet puts it: *We were sold into slavery for our sins.*[85] For whenever a man indulges his lusts, he sells his soul for a price. Under that bond, then, every man was tied in bondage to those wicked rulers: but by His coming Christ tore it down and stripped them of this their power. This is what Paul is trying to explain, although wrapping it up in a great mystery, when he says of Him: *Blotting out the bond that was against us, . . . and . . . fastening it to His cross, He hath exposed principalities and powers, . . . triumphing over them in Himself.*[86] So those rulers, whom God had appointed over mankind, turning stubborn and tyrannical, did their best to wage war on the human beings committed to their charge and to rout them in their conflict with sin. The prophet Ezechiel points to this when he remarks, in mystical language: *In that day shall angels come forth hastening to destroy Ethiopia, and there shall be confusion among them in the day of Egypt; for, behold, He cometh.*[87] Thus Christ is said to have stripped them of their omnipotence and to have triumphed, restoring to men the power which had been wrested from them. He Himself explains this to His disciples in the Gospel: *Behold, I have given you power to tread upon serpents and scorpions and upon all the power of the Enemy.*[88]

So those who wickedly abused the authority they had received were brought into subjection to their sometime subjects by Christ's cross. As for us, the race of men, the cross teaches us, first of all, to resist sin to death, and gladly to lay down our lives for our religion. Secondly, He sets before us in this selfsame cross an example of obedience, just as He imposed penalties on the stubborn disobedience of our former rulers. Attend, therefore, to the words in which the Apostle tries to teach us obedience by means of Christ's cross: *Let this mind be in you*, he says, *which was in Christ Jesus, who, being in the form of God, thought it not robbery to be equal with God, but emptied Himself, taking the form of a servant, being made in the likeness of men, and in habit found as a man, was made obedient unto death, even to the death of the cross.*[89] So, being a consummate master, ever ready to practise what He taught, He reinforced His lesson that good men must render obedience even at the cost of their lives by laying down His own life in rendering it.

16. But perhaps some people find doctrine like this alarming because, whereas a few pages back I affirmed His coeternity with God the Father and His birth from His substance, teaching that He is one with God the Father in kingship, majesty, and everlastingness, now I am making His death my theme. But I would ask you, believing reader, not to yield to such alarm. A little later you will see Him, of whose death you are now hearing, once again immortal: the death to which He submits is going to result in the despoiling of death. For the motive behind the mystery of the incarnation, which I previously explained, was just this: the divine power of the Son of God, like a hook wrapped in a covering of human flesh and, as the Apostle Paul said, *in habit found as a man*, was to lure on the Prince of the World to a conflict, and while Christ

offered him His human flesh as a bait, the Deity concealed within was to hold him fast with a hook,[90] as a result of the shedding of His immaculate blood. Only He who Himself knows no stain of sin could abolish the sins of all men, at any rate of those who had marked the doorposts of their faith with His blood.[91] When a fish, for example, seizes a hook concealed in a bait, it not only cannot remove the bait from the hook, but is itself dragged out of the deep to become a bait for other fish. In precisely the same way, when he who had the power of death seized the body of Jesus, he failed to notice the hook of Deity enclosed within it: so, when he swallowed it, he was immediately caught and, bursting the bars of the underworld, was dragged out from the abyss to become a bait for others. That this would come about the prophet Ezechiel made manifest long ago, using the identical figure and saying: *And I will draw thee up with my hook, and I will stretch thee out on the earth; the fields will be filled with thee, and I will set all the birds of heaven over thee, and I will satiate all the beasts of the earth with thee.*[92] The prophet David also says: *Thou hast broken the heads of the great dragon, thou hast given him to be meat to the people of the Ethiopians.*[93] In similar fashion Job witnesses to the same mystery, representing the Lord as addressing him: *Or wilt thou lead the dragon with a hook, and wilt thou put a bit about his nostrils?*[94]

17. Consequently, Christ's suffering in His flesh entailed no loss or injury to His Deity. It was in order to accomplish salvation through the weakness of flesh that His divine nature went down to death in the flesh. The intention was, not that He might be held fast by death according to the law governing mortals, but that, assured of rising again by His own power, He might open the gates of death. It was as if a king were to go[95] to a dungeon

and, entering it, were to fling open its doors, loosen the fetters, break the chains, bolts, and bars in pieces, conduct the captives forth to freedom, and restore *such as sat in darkness and in the shadow of death*[96] to light and life. In a case like this the king is, of course, said to have been in the dungeon, but not under the same circumstances as the prisoners confined within it. They were there to discharge their penalties, but he to secure their discharge from punishment.

THE PASSION FORETOLD IN PROPHECY

18. Furthermore, those responsible for handing the creed down have shown great forethought in specifying the actual date of the events, UNDER PONTIUS PILATE,[97] as a precaution against any vagueness or uncertainty upsetting the tradition of what happened. In the creed of the Roman church, we should notice, the words DESCENDED TO HELL are not added, nor for that matter does the clause feature in the Eastern churches.[98] Its meaning, however, appears to be precisely the same as that contained in the affirmation BURIED. No doubt, inspired as you are by loving devotion to the Sacred Scriptures, you will protest to me that these facts ought to be corroborated by convincing Scriptural evidence: the weightier the statements we are asked to believe, the more they call for appropriate, unambiguous testimony. There is truth and logic in the claim. On the assumption, however, that my argument is addressed to people familiar with the Law, I am deliberately passing over a whole forest of evidence for the sake of brevity. Still, if you demand it, I am ready to produce a few samples out of many,

knowing that keen researchers will find a vast ocean of testimony lying open to them in Holy Scripture.

19. We should realize, then, first of all, that the cross is not regarded by all in the same light: it means one thing to pagans, another to Jews, a third to believers. As the Apostle remarks: *But we preach Christ crucified: unto the Jews indeed a stumbling block, and unto the Gentiles foolishness, but unto them that are called, both Jews and Greeks, Christ, the power of God and the wisdom of God*; and, in the same context: *For the word of the cross, to them indeed that perish, is foolishness: but to them that are saved, that is, to us, it is the power of God.*[99] The Jews, relying on the tradition of their Law that the Christ would abide for ever, found His cross a stumbling block, for they were reluctant to admit His resurrection. To the Gentiles, ignorant as they were of the mystery of the incarnation, it seemed foolishness that God should have submitted to death. But Christians, with their firm belief in His birth, His passion in His human flesh, and His resurrection from the dead, with good reason accepted Him as the power of God which had vanquished death.

In the first place, then, this paradoxical fact, that these truths were to win credence, not among the Jews who had been informed of them in advance by the prophets, but among people to whom no prophets had ever mentioned them,[100] was hinted at prophetically by Isaias, as you can gather from his words: *They to whom it was not spoken of shall see: and they that have not heard shall understand.*[101] Isaias also foretold the unbelief of the nation which had meditated upon God's Law from childhood to age, and the transference of the whole providential purpose from them to the Gentiles, prophesying as follows: *And the Lord God of Sabaoth shall make a feast unto all the Gentiles on this mountain: they shall drink joy, they shall drink wine, they shall be anointed with ointment on this mountain. Hand over all these things to the Gentiles. For such is the counsel of the Almighty in regard to all the Gentiles.*[102] Possibly the nation which boasts of its knowledge of the Law will object to me, saying: 'You speak blasphemously when you allege that the Lord was made subject to the corruption of death and the passion of the cross.' In that case read what stands written for you in Jeremias's Lamentations: *The Spirit of our countenance, Christ the Lord, has been caught in our corruptions: of whom we said, Under His shadow we shall live among the Gentiles.*[103] You hear how the prophet states that Christ, the Lord, has been caught, and has been delivered over to corruption for us, that is, for our sins. Since the Jewish people has remained steadfast in unbelief, the Gentiles have been placed, as he states, *under His shadow*, seeing that we live among the Gentiles, and not in Israel.

20. But if it does not strike you as tedious,[104] I shall indicate how the several incidents of the Gospel story were foretold in the prophets. In this way beginners, learning the basic elements of the faith, will have these evidences written out in their hearts, so that no insidious uncertainty may ever rob them of their beliefs. We are informed in the Gospel that one of Christ's friends and table companions, Judas, betrayed Him. Just listen to the prediction of this in the Psalms: *He who ate my bread has lifted up his heel against me.*[105] Elsewhere we read: *My friends and my neighbours have drawn near, and stood against me.*[106] Again: *His words are smoother than oil, and the same will be darts.*[107] Would you care to hear how they have been made smooth? *Judas came to Jesus*, it is written, *and said to Him, Hail, Rabbi; and he kissed Him.*[108] By means of the smooth blandishments of a kiss he thrust home the accursed dart of betrayal.

Thereupon the Lord said to him: *Judas, dost thou betray the Son of man with a kiss?*[109] Again, you are told that, as a result of the traitor's greed, He was priced at thirty pieces of silver. On this subject, too, listen to the voice of prophecy: *And I said to them, if it be good in your sight, give me my price; or else refuse.* Then in what follows: *I took the thirty pieces of silver, and cast them into the house of the Lord, into the foundry.*[110] Is not this the story told in the Gospels, how Judas, overcome with remorse, brought back the money, cast it into the temple, and went off?[111] Most aptly He called it *my price*, with an air of upbraiding and reproach. For He had done so many good works among them: He had healed their blind, and had given back their feet to the lame, their power of walking to the paralysed, and life itself to the dead. And for all this goodness they repaid Him with death—a death appraised at thirty pieces of silver! Again it is reported in the Gospels that He was bound. The voice of prophecy announced this through Isaias, saying: *Woe unto their soul: they have devised a wicked device against themselves, saying, Let us bind the Just One, for He is useless to us.*[112]

21. But there may be a protest: 'Surely we are not to interpret these texts as referring to the Lord? Surely the Lord could not be held prisoner by men, or be dragged to judgment?' On this point, too, the same prophet will convince you; for he uses these very words: *The Lord Himself will enter into judgment with the ancients and the princes of the people.*[113] So, according to the prophet's testimony, the Lord was judged, and not only judged, but beaten with scourges as well: He was slapped in the face by men's palms, He was spat upon, and He had to put up with every kind of insult and humiliation for our sakes. Indeed, it was because facts like these were bound to arouse incredulity

when proclaimed by the Apostles, that the prophet, speaking in their person, exclaimed: *Lord, who hath believed our reports?*[114] For it passes belief that God, the Son of God, should, as Christian preachers affirm, have suffered such indignities. In order, therefore, to prevent doubts arising among prospective believers, these things were announced beforehand by the prophets. Christ our Lord Himself, speaking in His own person, declared: *I have given my back to the scourges, and my cheeks to men's palms; and I have not turned away my face from the confusion of spitting.*[115]

Among His other sufferings Scripture records that they bound Him and led Him before Pilate. This also was fore-shadowed by the prophet in the words: *And they bound Him and brought Him as a present to King Jarim*—[116] unless someone is going to object and point out that Pilate was not a king. If so, listen to what the Gospel relates in the sequel: *Pilate heard that He was from Galilee, and sent Him to Herod, who was king in Israel at that time.*[117] There was point, moreover, in the addition of the name 'Jarim,' which signifies 'wild.'[118] For Herod did not belong to the house of Israel, or to that Israelite vine which the Lord brought up out of Egypt and planted *on a hill, in a fruitful place:*[119] he was rather a wild vine, that is, from a plantation of alien stock. So he was correctly called 'wild,' seeing that he could not claim to have sprung from the shoots of the vine of Israel. The prophet also neatly adapted the word 'present' to what he was saying. For Herod and Pilate were at that time, as the Gospel testifies, restored to harmony after being enemies, and each sent Jesus in chains to the other as a present in token of their reconciliation. But what does that matter, so long as Jesus, in His capacity as Saviour, reconciles the quarrelsome, restores peace, and also brings back harmony? There is a passage in Job dealing with this too: *The Lord reconciles the hearts of princes of the earth.*[120]

22. It is further related that, when Pilate wanted to release Him, the whole multitude shouted in uproar: *Crucify Him, crucify Him.*[121] This was foretold by the prophet Jeremias, speaking in the person of the Lord Himself: *My inheritance,* he says, *is become to me as a lion in the wood: it hath cried out against me. Therefore have I hated it. And therefore,* he adds, *I have forsaken my house.*[122] In yet another passage he says: *Upon whom have you opened your mouth wide, and against whom have you let loose your tongues?*[123] When He was being tried, Scripture reports that *He held His peace.*[124] Many passages bear witness to this. In the Psalms we read: *I became as a man that heareth not, and that hath no reproofs in his mouth.* Again: *I, as a deaf man, heard not, and as a dumb man not opening his mouth.*[125] Yet another prophet says: *As a lamb before its shearer, so He opened not His mouth. In His humiliation His judgment was taken away.*[126] A crown of thorns, it is written, was set upon Him. On this subject, too, listen to the voice of God the Father, in the Canticle of Canticles, expressing amazement at the wickedness of Jerusalem in so insulting His Son: *Go forth, ye daughters of Jerusalem, and see the crown with which His mother crowned Him.*[127] Another prophet mentions the thorns in these words: *And I looked that it should bring forth grapes, but it brought forth thorns, and instead of justice, a cry.*[128] If I may disclose to you, however, the heart of the mystery, it was appropriate that He who came to remove the sins of the world should at the same time release the earth from the curses inflicted on it when the first-formed man sinned, and it received the sentence of transgression in the Lord's words: *Cursed is the earth in thy works: thorns and thistles shall it bring forth to thee.*[129] Jesus was therefore crowned

with thorns in order that the primordial sentence of con-
demnation might be remitted. He was led to the cross, and
the life of the whole world hung suspended from its wood.
Would you care to have this, too, confirmed by the testimony of prophets? Listen to what Jeremias has to say
about it: *Come, and let us put wood upon His bread, and let
us cut Him off from the land of the living.*[130] Moses again,
lamenting over them, remarked: *And thy life shall be
hanging suspended before thine eyes, and thou shalt fear by day
and by night, neither shalt thou trust thy life.*[131]

I ought, however, to hurry on, having already exceeded
my self-imposed limits of brevity and having expanded
my *short word* into a lengthy treatise. But I shall add a few
points more, in case I should be thought to have entirely
passed over what I undertook. 23. According to Scripture,
then, when Jesus was pierced in His side, blood and water
poured out together.[132] There is a mystical significance in
this, for He Himself declared: *Out of his belly shall proceed
forth rivers of living waters.*[133] But the blood which He shed
forth was the blood which the Jews prayed might be upon
themselves and their children.[134] So He shed forth water
to cleanse believers; but His blood He shed forth to con-
demn unbelievers. We can equally well interpret this as
foreshadowing the twofold grace of baptism, the grace
which is bestowed by the baptismal water, and the grace
which is acquired by shedding one's blood in martyrdom;[135] for both are designated baptism. But if you go on
to inquire why He is said to have shed water and blood
from His side, and not rather from some other part of
His body, my conjecture is that His side with its rib mystically signifies a woman.[136] The fountainhead of sin and
death, you see, derived from the first woman, and she
had been the rib of the first Adam: so the fountainhead

of redemption and life derives from the rib of the second Adam.

24. It is written that during His passion darkness prevailed from the sixth to the ninth hour.[137] Let us cite the witness of the prophet to this also: *Thy sun shall go down at midday.*[138] The prophet Zacharias says similarly: *In that day there shall be no light. There shall be cold and frost in one day. And that day shall be known to the Lord, and it shall be neither day nor night. And towards evening there will be light.*[139] What plainer language could the prophet have used had he wanted his words to appear, not so much a prediction of the future, as a narrative of the past? He gave notice both of cold and frost. The reason for Peter's warming himself at the fire was that it was cold;[140] and the cold from which he suffered was not only the coldness of weather but coldness of faith. He adds: *And that day shall be known to the Lord; and it shall be neither day nor night.* What do the words, *neither day nor night*, mean? Surely he was making a pointed reference to the breaking in of darkness on the day and the subsequent restoration of light. That was not really day, for it did not begin with sunrise. It was not night in the full sense of the word either, since it did not embark on its proper course from the beginning, when day was over, nor did it bring it to its appointed completion. But the light, which had been driven away by the wickedness of impious men, was restored towards evening. After the ninth hour, you see, the darkness was dispelled, and the sun shone once more on the world. There is yet another witness to this in the words: *And the light will be made dark over the earth in the day.*[141]

25. The Gospel account further relates that the soldiers divided Jesus's clothes among themselves, and cast lots for His tunic.[142] This also the Holy Spirit made it His business

to announce beforehand by the mouth of prophets, for David says: *They parted my garments among them, and upon my vesture they cast lots.*[143] The prophets did not even fail to mention the garment the soldiers are reported to have dressed Him in out of mockery, I mean the scarlet robe. Just listen to what Isaias says: *Who is this that cometh from Edom? The redness of his garments from Bosra? . . . Why is thy apparel red, and thy raiment as though trodden in a winepress?*[144] He Himself replied to this: *I have trodden the winepress alone, daughters of Sion.*[145] For it is He alone who has committed no sin, and who has taken away the sin of the world. For if by one man death could enter the world, how much more could life be restored by one man, who was God as well?[146]

26. It is also reported that He was given vinegar to drink, or wine mixed with myrrh, which is more bitter than gall. Hear the prophet's words foretelling this: *And they gave me gall for my food, and in my thirst they gave me vinegar to drink.*[147] In harmony with this Moses, even in his day, remarked of that people: *Their vine is of the vineyard Sodom, and their vine-shoot of Gomorrah. Their grapes are of gall, and their clusters most bitter.*[148] On another occasion, rebuking them, he says: *Is this the return thou makest to the Lord, O foolish and senseless people?*[149] The same incident is anticipated in Canticles too, where the very garden of the crucifixion is foreshadowed: *I am come into my garden, O my sister, my spouse, and I have gathered my myrrh.*[150] Here the prophet has unambiguously hinted at the wine mixed with myrrh which He was given to drink.

27. Scripture next records that He *gave up the ghost.*[151] This also had been foretold by a prophet, speaking in the person of the Son addressing the Father: *Into Thy hands I commend my spirit.*[152] Tradition relates that He was buried,

and that a great stone was placed in the entrance to the sepulchre. Hear also what the voice of prophecy, by the mouth of Jeremias, predicted about this: *They have cast my life dead into a pit, and they have laid a stone over me.*[153] Here we have the most unmistakable pointers to His burial put forward in the prophet's words. But listen to other predictions as well: *The just man has been taken away from before the face of evil, and his place is in peace.*[154] Or take another passage: *And I shall give the wicked for his burial.*[155] Similarly another: *Resting he slept like a lion, and like a lion's whelp. Who shall awake him?*[156]

28. Furthermore, the fact that He descended to hell is unmistakably prophesied in the Psalms, where we read: *And thou hast brought me down in the dust of death.*[157] Or again *What profit is there in my blood when I shall go down into corruption?*[158] Or again: *I have gone down into the mire of the deep, and there is no standing.*[159] John for his part asked: *Art Thou he that art to come* (down to hell, no doubt)? *Or look we for another?*[160] That was why St. Peter wrote: *Because Christ, being put to death indeed in the flesh, but enlivened in the Spirit which dwells in Him, went down to preach to those spirits which were shut up in prison, which had been incredulous in the days of Noe.*[161] Incidentally, this passage makes plain the nature of the task He accomplished in the underworld. Moreover, the Lord Himself announced by the mouth of His prophet, as if speaking about the future: *Because Thou wilt not leave my soul in hell, nor wilt Thou give Thy Holy One to see corruption.*[162] This again He shows in prophetic language to have been actually fulfilled, when He says: *Thous hast brought forth, O Lord, my soul from hell: Thou hast saved me from them that go down into the pit.*[163]

CHRIST'S RESURRECTION

29. Next in order comes the clause, ON THE THIRD
DAY HE ROSE AGAIN FROM THE DEAD. The
glory of His resurrection brought out in Christ the
splendour of everything that previously seemed feeble
and weak. If a few moments ago you thought it impossible for One who was immortal to reach death, you
can now perceive the impossibility of His being mortal
who is declared to have vanquished death and to
have risen again. Herein you should discern the Creator's
goodness, in His readiness to follow you down to the
depths to which your sins have plunged you. You should
not, either, suggest that anything is impossible for God, the
Creator of all things, imagining that His work could have
been brought to an end by falling into an abyss to which
He could not penetrate in order to accomplish salvation.
'Underworld' and 'upper world' are terms which we
employ, limited as we are by the fixed circumference of
our bodies and confined within the limits of the space
assigned to us. But what is underworld or upper world to
God, who is present everywhere and is nowhere absent?
Notwithstanding, when He assumed a body, those dimen-
sions found their place. The flesh which had been laid in
the tomb was resuscitated in fulfilment of the prophet's
words: *Because Thou wilt not . . . give Thy Holy One to see
corruption.*[164] So He returned victoriously from the dead,
bringing with Him spoils from hell. For He conducted
forth those whom death held prisoners, [165] as He Himself
had prophesied in the words: *When I am lifted up from the
earth, I will draw all things to myself.*[166] The Gospel bears
witness to this when it states: *The graves were opened, and
many bodies of the saints that slept arose, and they appeared*

to many, and entered into the holy city.[167] By this is meant, I am sure, the city intended by the Apostle when he wrote: *But that Jerusalem which is above is free: which is mother of us all.*[168] He made the same point again to the Hebrews: *For it became Him for whom are all things, and by whom are all things, who had brought many children to glory, to perfect the author of their salvation by His passion.*[169] By His passion, therefore, He made perfect that human flesh which had been brought down to death by the first man's sin, and restored it by the power of His resurrection: sitting on God's right hand, He placed it in the highest heavens. In view of this the Apostle says: *Who hath raised us up together, and hath made us sit together in the heavenly places.*[170] It was He, you see, who was the potter mentioned by the prophet Jeremias: *The vessel which had fallen from His hand and was broken, He again raised up with His hands and formed anew, as it seemed good in His eyes.*[171] So it seemed good to Him to raise the mortal and corruptible body He had assumed from the rocky tomb, and rendering it immortal and incorruptible to place it, no longer in an earthly environment, but in heaven at His Father's right hand.

The Old Testament Scriptures are full of these mystery-laden allusions. No prophet, no lawgiver, no psalmist[172] is silent on this theme: almost without exception, the sacred pages all refer to these events. Hence it seems superfluous for us to linger collecting testimonies. I shall, however, set down just a few, referring anyone who craves for a fuller draught to the wellsprings of the inspired books themselves.

30. Thus in the Psalms, at the beginning, we find the remark: *I have slept and have taken my rest: and I have risen up, because the Lord hath protected me.*[173] Again, in another passage: *By reason of the misery of the needy and the groans of the poor, now will I arise, saith the Lord.*[174] Elsewhere, too, as

I pointed out above: *Thou hast brought forth, O Lord, my soul from hell: Thou hast saved me from them that go down into the pit.*[175] In yet another passage: *For turning Thou hast brought me to life, and hast brought me back again from the depth of the earth.*[176] A most explicit reference to Him is to be found in the eighty-seventh Psalm: *And He is become as a man without help, free among the dead.*[177] He does not phrase it, *a man,* but, *as a man.* For He was *as a man* when He descended to hell; but He was *free among the dead* in that death could not hold Him. Thus in one of His natures we see human weakness displayed, in the other, the power of divine majesty. Furthermore, the prophet Osee makes an unmistakable allusion to the third day in the words: *He will heal us after a two days' interval: yea, on the third day we shall rise again, and shall live in His sight.*[178] He utters this prophecy in the person of those who rise with Him on the third day, being restored from death to life. These are the people who say: . . . *on the third day we shall rise again, and shall live in His sight.* Isaias, for his part, has an unambiguous statement: *Who brought again from the earth the great Pastor of the sheep.*[179] In addition, Isaias prophesied that the women would witness His resurrection while the Scribes, Pharisees, and people would refuse to believe, saying: *You women who come from the spectacle, come: for it is not a people having understanding.*[180] There is also a prophecy about the women who, after His resurrection, are reported to have gone to the tomb in search of Him, without finding Him, like Mary Magdalene, who, according to the account, arrived at the sepulchre before dawn and, when she could not find Him, burst into tears and said to the angels standing by: *Because they have taken away the Lord, and I know not where they have laid him.*[181] The prophecy of this incident comes in Canticles: *In my bed I sought Him whom my soul loved: in the nights I sought Him, and found Him not.*[182] There is also in Canticles a prediction pointing to those who found Him and clasped His feet: *I will hold Him, and I will not let Him go whom my soul hath loved.*[183] These are a few passages selected from a large number: since my aim is brevity, I am prevented from adding to my collection.

THE ASCENSION AND SESSION

31. HE ASCENDED TO HEAVEN, HE SITS AT THE RIGHT HAND OF THE FATHER: THENCE HE WILL COME TO JUDGE LIVING AND DEAD. These clauses, coming at the end of the article, are expressed with fitting brevity. The affirmations they make are clear enough: what demands explanation is the sense in which they ought to be understood. For unless our interpretation of ASCENDED, SITS, and WILL COME consorts with the dignity of the Godhead, we shall suppose them to convey a suggestion of human weakness.[184] When Christ had completed His earthly career, and had rescued the souls from imprisonment in hell, it is stated that He ascended to heaven, thereby fulfilling the prophet's words: *Ascending on high, He led captivity captive: He gave gifts to men.*[185] The gifts meant are those of which Peter spoke in the Acts of the Apostles, referring to the Holy Spirit: *Being exalted, therefore, by the right hand of God, . . . He hath poured forth this gift which you see and hear.*[186] He gave, therefore, the gift of the Holy Spirit to men in that, whereas the devil had by sin dragged men captive down to hell, Christ by His rising from the dead restored them to heaven. But in ascending to heaven He did not go to a place where God the Word had not previously been, for

He existed eternally in heaven abiding in His Father, but
to a place where the Word made flesh had not been seated
before. Further, since His entry through the gates of heaven
struck its doorkeepers and princes as something novel, and
they saw fleshly nature penetrating the secret recesses of
heaven, they uttered to one another the words which
David, under the Holy Spirit's influence, foretold: *Lift up
your gates, O ye princes, and be ye lifted up, O eternal gates:
and the King of Glory shall enter in. Who is this King of
Glory? The Lord who is strong and mighty, the Lord mighty in
battles.*[187] This exclamation was not provoked by the
might of the Godhead, but by the unwonted sight of flesh
ascending to God's right hand. In another passage David
says similarly: *God is ascended with jubilation, and the Lord
with the sound of trumpet.*[188] For conquerors are accustomed
to return from battle with the sound of trumpets. That
other saying also refers to Him: *Who buildeth His ascension
in heaven.*[189] So also does the passage: *Who hath ascended
upon the Cherubim: He hath flown upon the wings of the
winds.*[190]

32. Furthermore, His sitting AT THE RIGHT HAND
OF THE FATHER is a mystery which is bound up with
His taking of flesh. On the one hand, apart from that
taking of flesh, the affirmation hardly accords with the
incorporeal nature of Godhead; and, on the other, the
perfection of being seated in heaven is something to be
sought for His human, not His divine, nature.[191] Hence it is
said of Him: *Thy throne is prepared, O God, from of old:
Thou art from everlasting.*[192] From everlasting, you see, the
throne had been prepared on which the Lord Jesus was to
sit, *in whose name every knee should bow, of those that are in
heaven, on earth, and under the earth, and every tongue should
confess to Him that the Lord Jesus is in the glory of God the*

Father.[193] David also has a reference to this: *The Lord said to my Lord: Sit Thou at my right hand, until I make Thy enemies Thy footstool.*[194] The Lord explained these words in the Gospel when He remarked to the Pharisees: *If David then call Him Lord in spirit, how is He His son?*[195] By this He revealed that He was Lord in His spirit, but David's son in respect of His flesh. So the Lord Himself again says: *Nevertheless, I say unto you, hereafter you shall see the Son of man sitting on the right hand of the power of God.*[196] The Apostle Peter says in reference to Christ: *Who is on the right hand of God, . . . seated in the heavens.*[197] Paul, too, writing to the Ephesians, remarks: *According to the operation of the might of His power, which He wrought in Christ, raising Him up from the dead and making Him sit at His right hand.*[198]

THE SECOND COMING AND JUDGMENT

33. As for His coming to judge living and dead, the truth of this is guaranteed for us by numerous testimonies in Holy Scripture. But before citing the predictions contained in prophecy, I think it necessary to remind you of the intention behind the doctrine, namely, that we should be daily apprehensive of the coming of the Judge. We are to frame our behaviour on the assumption that we shall have to give an account to a Judge who is at hand. This is what the prophet meant by his saying about the man who is blessed: *Forasmuch as he orders his words with judgment.*[199] But the statement that He will judge living and dead does not imply that some will come to the judgment alive and others dead. Rather it means that He will judge men's souls and bodies simultaneously, their souls being described as living and their bodies as dead.[200] The

Lord Himself speaks in similar vein in the Gospel, declaring: *Fear ye not them that can kill the body, but are not
able to do anything to the soul; but rather fear him that can
destroy both soul and body in hell.*[201]

34. Let me now briefly, if you are agreeable, show how
these things were foretold by the prophets: you will be
able to collect many more testimonies for yourself from
the length and breadth of Scripture. The prophet Mala-
chias, for example, says: *Behold, the Lord almighty shall come,
and who shall endure the day of His coming, or who shall endure
His aspect? For He approaches like the fire of a refining furnace,
and like the herb of them that wash clothes; and He shall sit
refining and cleansing as it were silver and as it were gold.*[202]
But for more certain evidence of the identity of this Lord
of whom these words are uttered, listen to the prophet
Daniel's prediction: *I beheld, he says, in the vision of the night,
and lo, one like the son of man coming with the clouds of heaven.
And he came even to the Venerable of days, and was presented
in his sight. And there was given unto him dominion, and
honour, and a kingdom; and all peoples, tribes, and tongues shall
serve him. And his power is an everlasting power that shall not
be taken away, and his kindom shall not be destroyed.*[203] From
these verses we gain information not only about His
coming and judgment, but also about His power and
kingdom. His power, we are told, is everlasting, and His
kingdom exempt from ending in destruction, as the Creed
itself affirms: AND OF HIS KINGDOM THERE
SHALL BE NO END.[204] Anyone, therefore, who declares
that Christ's kingdom will have to be brought to an end
some day, is a total stranger to the faith. We ought to
realize, however, that, in his desire to deceive the faithful,
the Enemy attempts crafty devices to counterfeit this
gracious coming of Christ's. Instead of the Son of Man,

whose coming in the majesty of His Father is eagerly awaited, he sends ahead the son of perdition with prodigies and lying signs, trying to introduce Antichrist to the world in place of Christ. It was with him in mind that the Lord remarked in the Gospels to the Jews: *Because I am come in the name of my Father, and ye have received me not, another shall come in his own name, and him ye shall receive.*[205] In another passage He says: *When you shall see the abomination of desolation standing in the holy place, as Daniel the prophet foretold: he that readeth, let him understand.*[206]

In his visions Daniel gives abundant and detailed information about the coming of this delusion, but it would be tedious to set down instances now: I have already enlarged on the subject at sufficient length. I would refer anyone desirous of fuller knowledge to the visions themselves. The Apostle, however, remarks about Antichrist: *Let no man deceive you by any means, for unless there come a revolt first, and the man of sin be revealed, the son of perdition who opposeth and is lifted up above all that is called God or that is worshipped, so that he sitteth in the temple of God, showing himself as if he were God.*[207] Again, a little later: *And then the wicked one shall be revealed, whom the Lord Jesus shall kill with the spirit of His mouth, and He shall make Him void with the brightness of His coming; whose coming is according to the works of Satan, in all power, signs, and lying wonders.*[208] A little later, in similar vein: *And therefore God shall send them the operation of error, to believe lying: that all may be judged who have not believed the truth.*[209] The reason for the proclamation of this delusion to us through the mouths of prophets, evangelists, and apostles is to prevent anyone from mistaking the coming of Antichrist for Christ's coming. As the Lord Himself says: *When they shall say to you, Lo here is Christ, or, Lo there, do not believe them. For there shall come many false Christs and false prophets, and they shall lead many astray.*[210] Let us observe, however, the proofs He has given of the judgment of the authentic Christ: *As lightning shineth from the East even unto the West, so shall the coming of the Son of man be.*[211] When the authentic Lord Jesus Christ comes, therefore, He will take His seat and will set up His judgment, as He Himself declares in the Gospels: *And He shall separate the sheep from the goats,*[212] that is, the just from the unjust. So the Apostle writes: *Because we must all stand before the judgment seat of Christ, that every one may receive the proper things of the body, according as he hath done, whether they be good things or evil.*[213] The judgment will be passed, moreover, with an eye not only to our deeds, but to our thoughts as well, as the Apostle also indicated: . . . *their thoughts between themselves accusing or also defending one another, in the day in which God shall judge the secrets of men.*[214]

THE HOLY SPIRIT

35. Let this be enough on this subject. Next in the order of belief comes, AND IN THE HOLY SPIRIT. The detailed, rather lengthy account of Christ recorded above has reference to the mystery of His incarnation and passion. Being taken in connection with His person, it has formed an interruption which has held up my discussion of the Holy Spirit.[215] If our theme were exclusively the Godhead, we should say at the outset, I BELIEVE IN GOD THE FATHER ALMIGHTY, and then, IN JESUS CHRIST, HIS ONLY SON, OUR LORD: then in exactly the same way we should, without more ado, append, AND IN THE HOLY SPIRIT. All the intervening allusions to Christ, as I have pointed out,

are concerned with His incarnate state. Consequently, we complete the mystery of the Trinity with our mention of the Holy Spirit. Just as we speak of the Father as one, there being no other Father, and of the only-begotten Son as one, there being no other only-begotten Son, so the Holy Spirit is also one, and there can be no other Holy Spirit.[216] In order to bring out the distinction of Persons, you see, we employ separate terms expressive of relationship. Thus, He is to be taken as Father from whom are all things, and who Himself has no Father. The Second Person is to be regarded as Son, in virtue of His being born from the Father. The Third is the Holy Spirit, inasmuch as He proceeds from the mouth of God[217] and sanctifies all things. At the same time, to emphasize the unity and identity of the Godhead in the Trinity, just as we say we believe IN GOD THE FATHER, prefixing the preposition IN, so we use the form IN CHRIST, HIS SON, and also IN THE HOLY SPIRIT.[218] The meaning of what I have said will, however, be made plainer in the sequel.

36. Immediately after this clause follow the words, THE HOLY CHURCH, THE REMISSION OF SINS, THE RESURRECTION OF THIS FLESH. The creed does not say: IN THE HOLY CHURCH, or IN THE REMISSION OF SINS, or IN THE RESURRECTION OF THE FLESH. Had the preposition IN been inserted, the force of these articles would have been identical with that of their predecessors.[219] As it is, in the clauses in which our faith in the Godhead is laid down, we use the form, IN GOD THE FATHER, IN JESUS CHRIST HIS SON, and IN THE HOLY SPIRIT. In the other clauses, where the theme is not the Godhead but created beings and saving mysteries, the preposition IN is not interpolated. Hence we are not told to believe IN THE HOLY CHURCH, but

that the Holy Church exists, speaking of it not as God, but as a Church gathered together for God. So Christians believe, not *IN* THE REMISSION OF SINS, but that there is a remission of sins, and not *IN* THE RESURRECTION OF THE FLESH, but that there is a resurrection of the flesh. Thus the effect of this monosyllabic preposition is to distinguish the Creator from His creatures, and to draw a boundary line between things divine and things human.

It was this Holy Spirit, then, who inspired the Law and the Prophets in the Old Testament, and the Gospels and the Apostles in the New. So the Apostle remarks: *All Scripture, inspired of God, is profitable to teach.*[220] Consequently, it seems appropriate at this point, basing myself on the records of the Fathers,[221] to enumerate the books of the Old and New Testaments which, according to the tradition of our forefathers, are believed to have been inspired by the Holy Spirit Himself and to have been entrusted by Him to the churches of Christ.

THE SACRED CANON

37. In the Old Testament, then, first of all five books by Moses have been handed down—Genesis, Exodus, Leviticus, Numbers, and Deuteronomy; then Josue, the son of Nun, and Judges, together with Ruth;[222] then four books of Kings, reckoned by the Jews as two;[223] Paralipomenon, otherwise called the Book of Days;[224] two books of Esdras, which the Jews count as one;[225] and Esther.[226] Of prophets we have Isaias, Jeremias, Ezechiel, and Daniel, and, in addition, a single book of the Twelve Prophets.[227] Job, also, and the Psalms of David are each of them one book. There are three which Solomon bequeathed to the

churches, namely, Proverbs, Ecclesiastes, and the Canticle of Canticles. With these they completed the list of books belonging to the Old Testament.

In the New [228] there are four Gospels, those of Matthew, Mark, Luke, and John; the Acts of the Apostles, composed by Luke; fourteen Epistles by the Apostle Paul; two by the Apostle Peter; one by James, brother of the Lord and Apostle;[229] one by Jude; three by John; and the Apocalypse of John.

38. These are the writings which the Fathers included in the canon,[230] and on which they desired the affirmations of our faith to be based. At the same time we should appreciate that there are certain other books which our predecessors designated 'ecclesiastical'[231] rather than 'canonical.' Thus, there is the Wisdom of Solomon, as we call it; and another Wisdom, ascribed to the son of Sirach.[232] This latter is known by the general title Ecclesiasticus[232] among Latin-speaking people, the description pointing, not to the author of the book, but to the character of the writing. The Book of Tobias belongs to the same class, as do Judith and the books of the Machabees.[233] In the New Testament we have the little work known as The Book of the Shepherd, or Hermas,[234] and the book which is named The Two Ways,[235] and The Judgment of Peter.[236] They desired that all these should be read in the churches, but that appeal should not be made to them on points of faith. The other writings they designated 'apocryphal,'[237] refusing to allow them to be read out in church. Such, then, is the traditional canon handed down to us by the Fathers. As I remarked above, I have thought this the proper place to draw attention to it for the information of catechumens receiving their first lessons in the Church and its faith, so that they may be in no doubt about the wellsprings

from which their draughts of the word of God must be taken.

THE HOLY CHURCH

39. The next clause in the ordered statement of our faith runs, THE HOLY CHURCH.[238] I have already explained in what precedes why they did not say *IN* THE HOLY CHURCH at this point too. So the faithful, having had the belief in one God mysteriously triune inculcated in the foregoing sections, are now in addition required to believe in the existence of one holy Church, a Church, that is, in which there is one faith and one baptism, and in which we believe in one God the Father, one Lord Jesus Christ His Son, and one Holy Spirit.

This, then, is what we mean by the Holy Church, which is *without spot or wrinkle*.[239] There are many others who have formed churches: for example, Marcion, Valentinus, Ebion, Mani, Arius, and the rest of the heretics.[240] These churches of theirs, however, are not without the spot or wrinkle of treachery. Hence the prophet's comment on them: *I have hated the assembly of the malignant, and with the wicked I will not sit.*[241] But listen to what the Holy Spirit, in Canticles, says about this Church of ours, which holds fast to the entire Christian faith: *One is my dove; one is she; and perfect unto her mother.*[242] Hence the man who embraces this faith in the Church should not go astray in the *council of vanity*, or enter in with *doers of unjust things*.[243] The *council of vanity* denotes Marcion's assembly, denying as he does that the Father of Christ is God the Creator who made the world by the agency of His Son.[244] The *council of vanity* stands for Ebion's teaching that our faith in Christ should involve the maintenance of the circumcision of the flesh, sabbath-keeping, the sacrificial system, and all the other observances prescribed by the letter of the Law.[245] The *council of vanity* describes Mani's teaching, in the first place because he called himself the Paraclete, and, in the second place, because he declares the world to have been made by an evil deity. He denies that God is the creator, rejects the Old Testament, and asserts the existence of two mutually antagonistic orders of reality, one good and the other evil. Men's souls, he affirms, are coeternal with God and, in harmony with Pythagorean views, return by varying cycles of generation into cattle, animals, and wild beasts. He denies the resurrection of our flesh, and lays it down that the Lord's passion and nativity took place only in appearance, and not in physical actuality.[246] The *council of vanity* stands for the contention of Paul of Samosata and of his successor, Photinus, that, so far from being begotten of the Father before the ages, Christ took His origin from Mary, and for their theory of Him, not as God born as man, but as a man elevated to deity.[247] The *council of vanity* stands for the doctrine of Arius and Eunomius, who want the Son of God to have been created out of nothing, instead of having been begotten from the Father's very substance, thereby implying that the Son of God had a beginning and is inferior to the Father. In similar vein they declare the Holy Spirit to be not only inferior to the Son, but no more than His deputy.[248] The *council of vanity* describes the opinion of those who, while confessing that the Son is of the Father's substance, place the Holy Spirit in a separate category, [249] in spite of the Saviour's having demonstrated in the Gospel the unity and indivisibility of the Trinity in the words: *Baptize all nations in the name of the Father and of the Son and of the Holy Spirit.*[250] Clearly it is blasphemous for a man to put asunder what has been joined together by God. The *council of vanity* also denotes the sect which some time ago collected round the obstinate, perverse suggestion that, while Christ assumed human flesh, He did not take a rational soul as well, in spite of the fact that the flesh, animal soul, reason, and mind of man have had one and the same salvation bestowed upon them by Christ.[251] The *council of vanity*, furthermore, includes both the sect which Donatus formed in Africa by accusing the Church of surrendering the sacred books, [252] and the one which Novatus stirred up by refusing the opportunity of penance to lapsed people, and by passing sentence on second marriages, even where necessity enjoins their contraction.[253]

Keep clear of all these, treating them as congregations of the malignant. Keep clear also of those—if indeed such are to be found—who are alleged to say that the Son of God does not possess the same vision and knowledge of the Father as the Father does of Him, or that Christ's kingdom must have an end, or that the resurrection of the flesh does not entail the complete restoration of its substance; and, similarly, of those who deny the universality of God's righteous judgment, and who believe that the devil will be absolved from the damnation which is his desert. The ears of the faithful, I repeat, should be deaf to all such.[254] Hold fast, on the other hand, to the HOLY CHURCH, which proclaims its faith in God the Father almighty, and His only Son Jesus Christ our Lord, and the Holy Spirit, as existing in one harmonious and indivisible substance, and believes that the Son of God was born from the Virgin, suffered for man's salvation, and rose again from the dead in the identical flesh with which He was born.

THE FORGIVENESS OF SINS

Further, the Church looks forward to His future coming as the universal judge, and preaches FORGIVENESS OF SINS[255] and RESURRECTION OF THE FLESH through Him.

40. As regards the FORGIVENESS OF SINS, our bare act of faith ought to be sufficient. Who would search for cause or explanation where a prince's bounty is in question? An earthly monarch's generosity is scarcely a fit subject for argument: then is God's largess going to be argued about by presumptuous humans? Pagans habitually make fun of us, [256] saying that we deceive ourselves if we imagine that mere words can wipe out offences which have actually been committed. 'Is it possible,' they say, 'for one who has committed murder to be no murderer, or for the perpetrator of adultery to be represented as no adulterer? How then is someone who is guilty of misdeeds like these going to be suddenly made holy?'

Faith, as I have pointed out, supplies a better answer to such charges than reason. He who has promised forgiveness is King of all things: He who assures us of it is Lord of heaven and earth. Are you reluctant for me to believe that He who made me a man out of mere clay can transform my guilt into innocence? Will He who caused me to see when I was blind and to hear when I was deaf, and who restored my powers of walking when I was lame, prove incapable of recovering my lost innocence for me? But we can appeal to nature's own testimony. Killing a man is not always heinous, but killing him illegally, out of evil intent, is heinous. What damns me, then, in such cases is not the deed done, for it can on occasion be done with propriety, but the mind's evil suggestion.[257] But if my mind should be put right again after having been guilty and having served as the source of wickedness, why should you assume that, because I was once guilty, I cannot be made innocent again? It is obvious, as the example quoted above proves, that the essence of guilt is the will, not the deed. If that is so, just as my wicked will brings me under the power of sin and death at the instigation of the evil demon, so that same will, by changing for the better, restores me to innocence and life at the prompting of the good God. The situation is identical in all other crimes. From this point of view no contradiction can be discovered between our faith and natural reason, so long as we understand the remission of sins to apply, not to the deeds done, which cannot be altered, but to the mind, which can undoubtedly be changed from bad to good.

THE RESURRECTION OF THE FLESH

41. The final clause, proclaiming as it does the RESURRECTION OF THE FLESH, rounds off the sum of all perfection with succinctness and brevity.[258] Even so, the Church's faith has to meet attacks on this point from heretics as well as pagans. Valentinus, for example, denies the resurrection of the flesh altogether; so do the Manichaeans, as I have already pointed out.[259] Such people have refused to listen to the prophet Isaias's words: *The dead shall rise again, and they who are in their graves shall be raised;*[260] or to wise Daniel's affirmation: *For then they who are in the dust of the earth shall rise again, these unto life everlasting, but these unto reproach and everlasting confusion.*[261] Even from the Gospels, which they appear to regard as authoritative, they ought to have learned what Our Lord and Saviour said when He was instructing the Sadducees:

But that the dead rise again, have you not read how He saith to Moses in the bush, The God of Abraham, the God of Isaac, the God of Jacob? But He is not the God of the dead, but of the living.[262] In the same context, in what went before, He disclosed the nature and glory of the resurrection in the statement: *But in the resurrection of the dead they shall neither marry nor be married, but shall be as angels of God.*[263] Thus the power of the resurrection bestows the condition of angels on men. As a result, those who have been raised from the earth dwell no longer on the earth with brute beasts, but in heaven with angels, their purer fashion of life having fitted them for this privilege. This applies only to those individuals whose chaste behaviour in this world keeps their flesh uncontaminated, and so brings it into obedience to the Holy Spirit. Cleansing it thus from every stain of vice and allowing it to be transformed into spiritual glory by the power of sanctification, they have been counted worthy to have it admitted to the society of angels.

42. But unbelievers exclaim in protest: [264] 'Human flesh rots and disintegrates, or else is changed into dust: it is sometimes sucked under the sea and dispersed in the waves. How then can it be collected together and fashioned into a whole again, so that a man's body is formed afresh out of it?' First, we may make a provisional reply to them in St. Paul's words: *Senseless man, that which thou sowest is not quickened, except it die first. And that which thou sowest, thou sowest not the body that shall be, but a bare grain of wheat or of some other kind of seed. But God giveth it a body as He will.*[265] Can you not believe that that transformation which you observe taking place annually in the seeds you scatter on the earth will be accomplished in your flesh, which like seed is sown in the ground according to God's law?[266]

Why, I ask you, should you take such a restricted, feeble view of the divine power as to believe it impossible for the dust out of which each individual's flesh is composed, once it is dispersed, to be collected together and restored to its original form? Are you not prepared to admit the possibility when you see the ingenuity of mere mortals discovering veins of metal buried deep in the earth, or the expert's eye noticing gold where the inexperienced man's assumes nothing but earth? Is there any reason why we should not allow such power to Him who made man, seeing the heights to which the creature made by Him can attain? Human skill discovers that gold and silver have separate veins of their own, and that what on the surface looks like earth conceals within it vastly different veins of copper, iron, or lead. What right have we then to presume that, however widely dispersed the particles composing each individual's flesh may be, the divine power will be incapable of finding and distinguishing them?

43. Let us try, however, to suggest reasons drawn from nature to assist sceptical minds to accept these truths. Let us imagine[267] a man jumbling seeds of different sorts together and sowing them indiscriminately, scattering them at random on the field. Is it not the case that, wherever all these various seeds have been scattered, each of them will develop into the appropriate shoot of its species at the proper season, exactly reproducing its own shape and structure? It is the same with the substance of each individual's flesh: however strangely and widely it has been dispersed, it possesses within it the principle of immortality, for it is the flesh of an immortal soul. Hence, at the precise moment which, when the bodies were planted like seed in the earth, seemed suitable to the will of the true God, this principle gathers the several particles from the

earth and unites them with their own substance, restoring the identical structure which death previously destroyed. The result is that each soul has restored to it, not a composite or alien body, but the actual one it formerly possessed. That is why it becomes possible, in recompense for the struggles of the present life, for the flesh which has lived morally to be crowned along with its soul, and for the immoral flesh to be punished. In expounding the faith of the Creed my church endeavours to safeguard this, adding a single adjective to the clause which elsewhere reads RESURRECTION OF THE FLESH, and handing it down in the form RESURRECTION OF THIS FLESH.[268] The word THIS, of course, refers to the actual flesh of the Christian who recites the creed, marking his forehead with the sign of the cross.[269] The idea is that each of the faithful should realize that, if only he keeps his flesh clean from sin, it will be a vessel of honour, useful to the Lord and serviceable for every good work, whereas if he allows it to be sullied by sin, it will be a vessel of wrath fitted for destruction.

As for the splendour of the resurrection and the greatness of God's promised reward, anyone who desires fuller information will find allusions to it in almost all the sacred books. I shall mention a few of them at this point, simply by way of recalling them to your mind: they can form the conclusion of the treatise you asked me to write. The Apostle Paul, for example, supports the claim that our mortal flesh will rise again with arguments like the following: *But if there be no resurrection of the dead, then Christ Himself is not risen again. And if Christ be not risen again, our preaching is vain; your faith, likewise, is empty.*[270] A few verses later he says: *But now Christ is risen from the dead, the beginning of them that sleep. For by a man came death, and by a*

*man the resurrection of the dead. For as in Adam all die, so also
in Christ all shall be made alive. But every one in his own order:
the beginning, Christ; then they that are of Christ at His
coming. Afterwards the end.*[271] In what follows he adds:
*Behold, I tell you a mystery. We shall all indeed rise again, but
we shall not all be changed* (or, as we read in some copies,
*we shall all indeed sleep, but we shall not all be changed), in a
moment, in the twinkling of an eye, at the last trumpet: for the
trumpet shall sound, and the dead shall rise again incorruptible.
And we shall be changed.*[272] Whatever the correct reading
there may be, he writes in his letter to the Thessalonians:
*And I will not have you ignorant, brethren, concerning them
that are asleep, that you be not sorrowful, even as others who
have no hope. For if we believe that Jesus died and rose again,
even so them who have fallen asleep through Jesus will God
bring with Him. For this we say unto you in the word of the
Lord, that we who are alive, who are left at the coming of the
Lord, shall not prevent them who have slept. For the Lord
Himself shall come down from heaven with commandment, and
with the voice of an archangel and the trumpet of God; and the
dead who are in Christ shall rise first. Then we who are alive,
who are left, shall be taken up together with them in the clouds to
meet Christ, into the air. And so shall we be always with the
Lord.*[273]

44. You must not assume, however, that St. Paul is the
sole mouthpiece of these truths, as if his message were a
novelty. Listen to the prophet Ezechiel's prediction,
uttered long ago under the inspiration of the Holy Spirit:
*Behold, I will open your sepulchres, and will bring you out of
your sepulchres.*[274] Listen also to Job, who is so rich in
mystical language, unmistakably foretelling the resurrection of the dead: *A tree hath hope. For if it be cut down, it will
bear buds again, and its shoots will never fail. But if its root*

grow old in the earth, and its trunk die in the dust, it will flourish again through the scent of water, and it will put forth foliage like a young plant. But a man, if he should die, hath he departed? And a mortal man, if he should fall, shall he be no more?[275] In these words is he not, as it were, moved by a sense of honour and obviously rallying men and saying: 'Is mankind then so stupid? They see the trunk of a felled tree shooting up again from the earth, and a dead log showing signs of renewed life: cannot they imagine something happening to them analogous to what happens even to blocks of wood and to trees?' For proof that the sentence, *But mortal man, when he fall, shall he not rise again?* is to be read as a question, consult the verses which follow. He straightway adds: *For if a man die, he shall live.*[276] A moment later he remarks: *I shall await until I be made again.*[277] Elsewhere he makes the same point: *He shall raise again upon the earth my skin, which now drinks its fill of these things.*[278]

45. Thus much, then, in demonstration of the belief we profess in the Creed, THE RESURRECTION OF THIS FLESH. As for THIS, you observe how well its addition harmonizes with all my citations from Holy Scripture. What else, for example, is Job emphasizing in the passage I explained above, when he says: *He will raise again my skin, which now drinks its fill of these things*, that is to say, which has to put up with these sufferings? Is he not pointing in the plainest way to the resurrection of *this* flesh—the flesh, I mean, which in this world has to endure the anguish of tribulation and trial?[279] Or take the Apostle's statement: *For this corruptible must put on incorruption, and this mortal must put on immortality.*[280] Does it not suggest that he is somehow touching his own body and placing his finger upon it? *This* body, he is saying, which is now corruptible, will, through the grace of resurrection,

become incorruptible, and *this* frame, which is now mortal, will be clothed with immortal capacities.[281] Hence, just as *Christ, rising from the dead, dieth now no more: death shall no more have dominion over Him,*[282] so those who will rise again in Christ will be no longer subject to either corruption or death, not because they will have discarded their flesh, but because its status and character will have been altered. It will be a real body, therefore, which will rise from the dead incorruptible and immortal; and this applies to just men and sinners alike. In the case of just men it will be to enable them to abide for ever with Christ; in the case of sinners, so that they may discharge, without undergoing destruction, the penalties which are their due.

46. The just, I repeat, abide for ever with our Lord Christ: the proof of this I provided in a previous chapter[283] when I quoted the Apostle's statement: *Then we who are alive, who are left, shall together with them be taken up in the clouds to meet Christ, into the air: and so shall we be always with the Lord.* There is no need for astonishment that, as a result of their resurrection, the flesh of the saints is to be gloriously transformed, being suspended in the clouds and carried along in the air to meet God. The Apostle himself, explaining the benefits God bestows on those who love Him, remarks: *Who will transform the body of our lowness, so that it becomes conformable to the body of His glory.*[284] So there is no absurdity in the suggestion that the bodies of the saints will be raised up on the clouds into the air, seeing it is stated that they are to be refashioned on the model of Christ's body, which is set on the right hand of God. The Apostle brings out this point too, with reference either to himself or to others of like status or merit, when he says: *For He will raise us up together with Christ, and will make us sit alongside Him in the heavenly places.*[285] Since then, at the

resurrection of the just, God's saints have already been promised these blessings, and countless others of the same kind, we should not find it difficult to credit the predictions once made by the Prophets, to the effect that *The just shall shine as the sun, and as the brightness of the firmament, in the kingdom of God.*[286] For will anyone find it difficult to believe that they will possess the brightness of the sun, and will be adorned with the splendour of these stars and this firmament, seeing that the life and companionship of God's angels is being prepared for them in heaven, and seeing that we are told they are to be refashioned on the model of the glory of Christ's body? It is this glory, promised them by the Saviour's own voice, which the blessed Apostle has in mind when he says: *It is sown a natural body: it shall rise a spiritual body.*[287] For if it is true, as it assuredly is true, that God's mercy is going to unite just men and saints, one and all, in fellowship with the angels, He will with equal certainty change their bodies too into the glory of a spiritual body.

47. You should not, however, draw the conclusion that what is here promised runs counter to the body's natural constitution. It is our belief, founded on Scripture, that God took *the slime of the earth*[288] when He made man, and that to form the nature of our body He changed earth into flesh by His decree. If so, why should you think it absurd or contradictory that, just as we hold earth to have been promoted so as to form animal body, in exactly the same way we should believe animal body to have been promoted so as to form spiritual body?

You will find all these testimonies to the resurrection of the just, and a host of others like them, in Sacred Scripture. But sinners too, as I explained above, will have the state of incorruption and immortality granted to them at the resurrection. As God bestows this state on the just with a view to their everlasting glory, so He will bestow it upon sinners so as to prolong their confusion and punishment. That prophetic utterance to which I referred a few moments ago made this perfectly clear in the words: *And many shall rise again from the dust of the earth: some to everlasting life, but others to confusion and everlasting reproach.*[289]

SUMMARY AND CLOSING PRAYER

48. We should now appreciate the awful significance of the description of almighty God as Father, the mysterious sense in which our Lord Jesus Christ is regarded as His only Son, the completeness and perfection of His Spirit's designation as Holy, and the way in which the Blessed Trinity, while one in substance, nevertheless involves distinctions of relation and persons.[290] We have studied the meaning of the Virgin Birth, of the birth of the Word in human flesh, and of the mystery of the cross. I have tried to explain the point of our Lord's descent to hell, the glory of His resurrection and His deliverance of the souls imprisoned in hell, and the meaning of His ascent to heaven and of the expected advent of the Judge. I have emphasized the recognition which ought to be accorded to the Holy Church in opposition to the congregations of vanity, the number of books in the canon, the heretical sects which should be shunned, and the fact that in the forgiveness of sins there is no contradiction whatever between the divine freedom and the natural reason.[291] I have explained, further, that the resurrection of our flesh is guaranteed not only by prophecy, but also by the example of our Lord and Saviour Himself and by the logic of natural reason. But if we have grasped all these points as they are set out in the

traditional formula we have been expounding, then it is my prayer that the Lord would vouchsafe to me and all my hearers that, having kept the faith we have embraced and having finished our course, we may await the crown of justice which has been laid up for us, and, being delivered from confusion and everlasting reproach, may be found among those who rise again to eternal life: through Christ our Lord, through whom to God the Father almighty, along with the Holy Spirit, is glory and dominion for ever and ever. Amen.

NOTES

LIST OF ABBREVIATIONS

ACW   Ancient Christian Writers (Westminster, Md.—London 1946–).

CSEL   Corpus scriptorum ecclesiasticorum latinorum (Vienna 1866–).

DACL   Dictionnaire d'archéologie chrétienne et de liturgie (Paris 1907–).

DTC   Dictionnaire de théologie catholique (Paris 1903–50).

FXM   F. X. Murphy, *Rufinus of Aquileia* (345–411), *His Life and Works* (Washington 1945).

GCS   Die griechischen christlichen Schriftsteller der ersten drei Jahrhunderte (Leipzig 1897–).

JNDK   J. N. D. Kelly, *Early Christian Creeds* (London 1950).

JTS   *Journal of Theological Studies* (London–Oxford 1900–).

LCP   Latinitas Christianorum primaeva (Nijmegen 1932–).

PG   J. P. Migne, Patrologia graeca (Paris 1857–66).

PL   J. P. Migne, Patrologia latina (Paris 1844–55).

TU   Texte und Untersuchungen zur Geschichte der altchristlichen Literatur (Leipzig 1882–).

TWNT   G. Kittel, Theologisches Wörterbuch zum Neuen Testament (Stuttgart 1933–).

The Catechetical Lectures of St. Cyril of Jerusalem are printed in PG 33: in the notes which follow they will be cited without column references.

[1] For a full account of the dates, circumstances, etc. of Rufinus's career, see FXM.

[2] Cf. St. Jerome, *Ep.* 3. 5 (CSEL 54. 17): 'cum post Romana studia ad Rheni semibarbaras ripas eodem cibo, pari frueremur hospitio.'

[3] The general view, supported by M. Villain in *Nouvelle revue théologique* 64 (1937) 30 ff., is that Melania and Rufinus met in Italy and travelled together to the East. FXM (40 ff.) argues that this involves reading too much into the words of St. Paulinus of Nola (*Ep.* 28. 5: CSEL 29. 246): 'sanctae Melani spiritali via comitem.' There is certainly little enough solid evidence to suggest that their companionship began before they had both set foot in Egypt. It seems safest to reserve judgment.

[4] Nitria has been identified as the Wadi Natrûn, about 75 miles north-west of the modern Cairo. With Scete, which lay about a day's journey distant, it was the principal centre of the Antonian, or semi-eremitical, type of monasticism which, inaugurated there by Ammoun (see Socrates, *Hist. eccl.* 4. 23: PG 67. 509 ff.) about 350, flourished in the second half of the fourth century. The hermits were solitaries, living out of earshot of each other, but they assembled together for worship on the Sabbath and on Sunday. For Nitria, see C. Butler, *Historia Lausiaca*, 2. 187–90.

[5] Cf. the engaging picture painted by Palladius in *Historia Lausiaca* 46; also 54. St. Jerome draws a caricature of Rufinus's activities as a lecturer in *Ep.* 125. 18 (CSEL 56. 137 f.).

[6] A significant illustration of the unfortunate effect of St. Jerome's polemics on Rufinus's reputation is supplied by the sixth-century author of the decretal (falsely ascribed to Pope Gelasius) *De libris recipiendis et non recipiendis*: 'Rufinus was a religious man, and wrote many books for the use of the Church, and many commentaries on the Scriptures. But since blessed Jerome censured him in certain matters concerning the freedom of the will, we side with Jerome.' For the original, see TU 38. 4. 71.

[7] St. Augustine's embarrassment at the estrangement of the two friends comes out vividly in *Ep.* 73. 6 ff. (CSEL 34. 270 ff.): 'I was exceedingly sorry that such grievous discord had broken out between persons once so affectionately intimate, bound together by ties of friendship notorious in almost all the churches. . . . What trusting

hearts can now pour themselves out in mutual confidences with impunity? Into whose breast may confiding love now throw itself without reserve? What friend, in short, may not be dreaded as a possible future foe, if the breach we now deplore could arise between Jerome and Rufinus? . . . It is a great and lamentable miracle that you two should have fallen from so fine a friendship into your present hostility. It will be an even greater miracle, and a joyful one too, if from such hostility you can be restored to your former amity.' See also *Ep.* 82. 1 (CSEL 34. 351 f.).

⁸ Cf. his actual words: 'Quis enim ibi stilo locus est, ubi hostilia tela metuuntur, ubi in oculis est urbium agrorumque vastatio, ubi fugitur per marina discrimina et ne ipsa quidem absque metu habentur exilia? in conspectu etenim, ut videbas etiam ipse, nostro Barbarus, qui Regini oppidi miscebat incendia, angustissimo a nobis freto, quod Italiae solum Siculo dirimit, arcebatur' (GCS 30. 1).

⁹ Cf. *Praef. ad Ezech.* (PL 25. 16 f.): 'The scorpion now lies buried in Sicilian soil between Enceladus and Porphyrion, and the many-headed hydra has at last ceased from hissing against me. So an opportunity is vouchsafed me of expounding the Bible instead of having to counter the insidious attacks of heretics.'

¹⁰ For an explanation of his theory about the adulteration and interpolation of Origen's writings, see the preface to his translation of the *De principiis* (GCS 22. 4 f.). In his Epilogue to Pamphilus's Apology for Origen he was able to quote a letter by the great theologian himself complaining that his writings had been tampered with and his teaching falsified. On Rufinus as translator, cf. Sr. M. M. Wagner, *Rufinus, the Translator: a Study of his Theory and his Practice as illustrated in his Version of the Apologetica of St. Gregory Nazianzen* (Washington 1945); also H. de Lubac, *Histoire et esprit: l'intelligence de l'Écriture d'après Origène* (Paris 1940) 40–42.

¹¹ Many scholars, it should be stated, have argued that these two books were not in fact original work by Rufinus, but were translations of two books written by Gelasius of Caesarea. Cf. especially A. Glas, *Die Kirchengeschichte des Gelasios von Kaisareia* (Leipzig 1914). But this thesis has been rendered improbable by the discussion of P. Peeters in *Analecta Bollandiana* 50 (1932) 5–58, and of F. Diekamp, *Analecta Patristica* (Rome 1938) 16–32.

¹² See his *De incarnatione Domini* 7. 27 (CSEL 17. 385): 'Rufinus quoque . . . ita in expositione symboli de domini nativitate testatur: "filius enim," inquit, "dei nascitur ex virgine, non principaliter soli carni sociatus, sed anima inter carnem deumque mediante generatus."'

¹³ See his *De viris inlustribus* 17 (TU 14. 1. 68): 'Proprio labore . . .

exposuit idem Rufinus symbolum, ut in eius comparatione alii nec exposuisse credantur.'

[14] He put forward the suggestion in his *Historiae literariae Aquileiensis libri V* (Rome 1742) 383.

[15] Cf. PL 21 *ad loc.*

[16] See *Apol. ad Anast.* 3 and 4 (PL 21. 625), and *Apol. in Hieron.* I. 5–9 (PL 21. 544–547).

[17] The date of the *Lectures* can be determined by one or two incidental time-references which crop up in the text, especially the statement in *Cat.* 6. 20 that the heresy of Mani began seventy years before the date at which St. Cyril was speaking. This would give 347 or 348. We should note that, while modern scholarship has tended to throw doubt on the authenticity of the last five lectures (the *Mystagogical Catecheses*) and to attribute them to St. Cyril's successor in the see, Bishop John of Jerusalem (see T. Schermann, *Theologische Revue* 10 [1911] 575–579; W. J. Swaans, *Le Muséon* 55 [1942] 1–43: answered briefly by F. L. Cross, *St. Cyril of Jerusalem's Lectures on the Christian Sacraments* [London 1951] xxxviii f.), St. Cyril's authorship of the body of the *Catecheses* has been securely established.

[18] It was apparently called 'Interpretation of the Creed' (ἑρμηνεία τοῦ συμβόλου), or 'Exposition of the Instruction' (ἐξήγησις τοῦ μαθήματος). On the question, see F. Diekamp, *op. cit.* 38 f.

[19] Niceta's *Libelli instructionis* were published by A. E. Burn in his *Niceta of Remesiana, His Life and Works* (Cambridge 1905).

[20] The *Explanatio* is printed in PL 17. 1155–60. For its Ambrosian origin, cf. R. H. Connolly, JTS 47 (1946) 185 ff.

[21] The date of *De fide et symbolo* is October, 393. Cf. St. Augustine's own words in *Retract.* I. 16 (CSEL 36. 84): 'About the same time, in the presence of the bishops who were holding at Hippo a plenary council of the whole of Africa, and at their bidding, I delivered a discourse, although still only a priest, *The Faith and the Creed.* Several of them, who were particularly attached to me, pressed me to publish the sermon, and so I made it into a book.'

[22] *Sermons* 212, 213, 214, and 215 (PL 38. 1058–76).

[23] Attention was first drawn to the dependence of the *Commentarius* on the *Oratio catechetica* by F. Diekamp, *op. cit.* 27 n. 1.

[24] So F. Diekamp, *loc. cit.*

[25] Eusebius's letter is printed in PG 20. 1535—44. The best modern critical edition of the text is that given by H. G. Opitz in the Prussian Academy's *Athanasius Werke* III Pt. I, *Urkunden zur Geschichte des Arianischen Streites* (Berlin and Leipzig 1935) no. 22. Eusebius opens his letter with a promise to reproduce (a) the credal statement he handed

ın on his own account at the Council of Nicaea, that is, the Caesarean Creed, and (b) the symbol which the Council eventually, despite his own misgivings, ratified. It now seems certain that his motive for submitting the Caesarean Creed to the Council was not, as scholars formerly held, to provide a basis for any new creed that might be drafted, but so as to secure the rehabilitation of his own orthodoxy, which had been brought into question at the Council of Antioch held earlier in the same year. See JNDK 220–26.

[26] Because the convention that the creed must be kept secret from the uninitiated (the *disciplina arcani*) was in operation, St. Cyril did not quote the creed *in extenso*. For the text which can be reconstructed from his *Lectures*, see JNDK 183 f.

[27] The original has been most faithfully preserved, in a Latin dress, in the fifth-century MS known as the Verona Fragment. For the text, see E. Hauler's *Didascaliae apostolorum fragmenta latina* (Leipzig 1900) 110 f. It should be noted that the first of the three questions is missing from the Verona Fragment: it has to be conjecturally restored from other versions. The most authoritative English edition, providing both a translation and textual notes, is that of G. Dix—*The Apostolic Tradition* (London 1937) 36 f. For a discussion of the text of the creed, see (among others) R. H. Connolly, JTS 25 (1934) 131 ff.; B. Capelle, *Revue Bénédictine* 39 (1927) 35 ff.; H. Lietzmann, *Zeitschrift für die Neutestamentliche Wissenschaft* 26 (1927) 76 ff.; G. Dix, *op. cit.* ix f.; P. Nautin, *Je crois à l'Esprit Saint* (Paris 1947) 13–27; B. Botte, *Mélanges Joseph de Ghellinck* (Gembloux 1951) I. 189–200.

[28] Cf. ch. 3.

[29] See his *De Romanae ecclesiae symbolo apostolico vetere aliisque fidei formulis . . . diatriba* (London 1647). As J. de Ghellinck remarked (*Patristique et moyen âge* I [2.ed., Brussels and Paris 1949] 28), 'La contribution de Jacques Ussher (1647) est à la base de toutes les recherches contemporaines sur les origines du symbole romain.'

[30] For the text, see St. Epiphanius, *Haer.* 72. 3. 1 (GCS 37. 258).

[31] The chief, almost the only, criticism of Ussher's thesis came from the late F. J. Badcock: see his *The History of the Creeds* (London 1930 and 1938). Badcock's arguments have been severely handled by H. Lietzmann, *Zeitschrift für die Neutestamentliche Wissenschaft* 22 (1923) 258, and JNDK 105–111.

[32] The MSS in question are the Graeco-Latin uncial Laud. Gr. 35 of the Bodleian Library, Oxford, better known as Codex E of the Acts of the Apostles (*saec.* 6 or 7), and the eighth-century Cottonian MS 2 A XX, now in the British Museum. The Latin text of the creed

has been inserted on the back of the last page but one (226 *verso*) of the former.

³³ For a cursory survey of Western creeds, with quotations of the principal examples, see JNDK 172–81. The discussion there also includes a demonstration of the dependence of all Western creeds on the Old Roman Creed.

³⁴ For the *Scarapsus*, see PL 89. 1029 ff. For the best critical edition of the text is that contained in G. Jecker's *Die Heimat des heiligen Pirmin* (Münster i. W. 1927).

³⁵ For a full treatment of the question of the provenance of the present Apostles' Creed, and of the stages by which it achieved a monopoly in the West and was eventually accepted at Rome, see JNDK ch. 13.

³⁶ The relation between the Old Roman Creed as attested by Rufinus and Marcellus, and the baptismal questionnaire recorded by St. Hippolytus, has been discussed by B. Capelle, *Revue Bénédictine* 39 (1927) 33–45, and JNDK 113–19.

³⁷ For the earlier history of R, see JNDK 119 ff.

³⁸ Rom. 6. 17.

³⁹ The precise date of the Pope's commission is unknown, but the first instalment of the revision, consisting of the four Gospels, appeared in 383. Acts and the rest of the New Testament followed almost immediately. Apart from the Gospels, the revision seems to have been largely perfunctory, in spite of St. Jerome's claim (*Ep.* 71. 5: CSEL 55. 6) that he had 'restored the New Testament to the authority of the original Greek.' It was about the same time that he made his first revision of the Old Latin Psalter, basing his emendations this time on the Greek of the Septuagint (see *Praef. in lib. ps*: PL 29. 117 f.).

⁴⁰ St. Augustine may be cited as a moderate example of the attitude of St. Jerome's contemporaries. He seems to have welcomed the new version of the Gospels: see *Ep.* 71. 6 (CSEL 34. 253 f.). As regards the Old Testament, however, he held that the Septuagint was no less inspired than the Hebrew (cf. *De civ. Dei* 18. 43: CSEL 40. 336–38), and he deprecated any new translation, mainly through fear of the offence it might occasion to weaker brethren (cf. *Ep.* 28. 2: CSEL 34. 105 f.—dated 394). Cf. also *Epp.* 71 (date 403) and 82. 35 (date 405): CSEL 34. 248 ff. and 386). In the latter context he remarks that he had refused to allow St. Jerome's version to be read in church 'ne . . . magno scandalo perturbemus plebes Christi.'

⁴¹ Cf. *Apol. in Hier.* 2. 32 ff. (PL 21. 611 ff.).

⁴² For a discussion of Rufinus's practice in dealing with Scriptural

quotations in the *De principiis*, see G. Bardy's article in *Revue Biblique* N.S. 16 (1919) 106 ff.

[43] Cf. G. Bardy, *Revue Biblique* 29 (1920) 240.

[44] For a useful discussion of the subject, see M. Stenzel, 'Der Bibel-kanon des Rufin von Aquileja,' in *Biblica* 23 (1942) 43–61.

[45] J. Oulton has discussed Rufinus's treatment of Eusebius's remarks on the canon in JTS 30 (1929) 156–59; see also FXM 168 f.

[46] Cf. *Cat.* 4. 35.

[47] *Ep. heort.* 39 (PG 26. 1436–40).

[48] Cf. *Apol. in Hier.* 2.33 f. (PL 21. 611–13).

[49] Cf. St. Athanasius, *Ep. heort.* 39 (PG 26. 1436); St. Jerome, *Prologus galeatus* (PL 28. 547 f.—for the title see n. 59 below); Origen, *In ps.* 1 (PG 12. 1084). Origen's statement is preserved by Eusebius in *Hist. Eccl.* 6. 25 (Schwartz 244). In the same passage Eusebius quotes Origen's account of the Old Testament canon.

[50] For Ambrosiaster's views on the canon, see M. J. Lagrange, *Histoire ancienne du Canon du Nouveau Testament* (Paris 1933) 141 f.

[51] This was the third Council of Carthage. For the text of its decree, see PL 56. 428 f.: also Denzinger, *Enchiridion Symbolorum* (ed. 28) n. 92. The wording of the original runs: '. . . Actus Apostolorum liber unus, Pauli Apostoli epistolae tredecim, eiusdem ad Hebraeos una. . . .'

[52] The variations of St. Augustine's attitude have been carefully examined by Dom O. Rottmanner in *Revue Bénédictine* 18 (1901) 257 ff. In his earliest writings he cited the Epistle as by St. Paul, in his middle period he wavered between Pauline authorship and anonymity, while from 409 to 430 he regularly referred to it as anonymous.

[53] For the text of Pope Innocent's letter (*Ep.* 6. 7: date 405), see PL 20. 501 f. and C. H. Turner's article in JTS 13 (1911–12) 77–82: also Denzinger, *op. cit.* n. 96.

[54] E.g. M. Stenzel in the article cited above (n. 44), 55.

[55] For the text, see PG 26. 1437.

[56] Cf. *Cat.* 4. 35 and 36. In the former passage St. Cyril speaks of 'the apocryphal writings,' and bids his audience have nothing to do with them.

[57] For citations from Wisdom, see *Cat.* 9. 2, 9. 16, 16. 19; for citations from Ecclesiasticus, 6. 4, 11. 19, 13. 8, 22. 8.

[58] These words occur in *Praef. in lib. Sal.* (PL 28. 1242 f.). For an examination of St. Jerome's attitude, see E. Mangenot's article, 'Canon des Livres Saints,' DTC 2. 2 (1910) 1577 f. Any occasional inconsistency of which he may have seemed guilty was probably due either to his desire to placate Western opinion (cf. e.g. *Praef. in lib. Tob.*: PL 29. 23–26), or to his realization that the books in

question actually did feature in the currently accepted list of inspired writings.

[59] Cf. *Prol. gal.* in PL 28. 556: '. . . ut scire valeamus quidquid extra hos est inter ἀπόκρυφα esse ponendum. Igitur Sapientia, quae vulgo Salomonis inscribitur, et Iesu filii Syrach liber, et Iudith, et Tobias, et Pastor, non sunt in canone. . . .' The title *Prologus galeatus*, or 'helmed preface' (i.e. a preface in which one defends one's position), is St. Jerome's own description (cf. PL 28. 555) of the introduction which he prefixed to his translation of the Hebrew Scriptures and in which he expounded his doctrine of the Canon.

[60] So, e.g., E. Mangenot, *art. cit.* 1577.

TEXT

[1] Nothing is known of this Lawrence. For conjectures as to his identity, see Introd. The word translated 'Bishop' is *Papa* in the original. In the early centuries, so far from being restricted to the Roman pontiff, *Papa* (in Greek ὁ πάπας) was freely applied to any bishop. Derived from the classical Greek πάππας, it was an affectionate diminutive for 'father.' The *Passion of SS. Perpetua and Felicity* (date 202–203: see ch. 13, ed. by J. A. Robinson in *Texts and Studies* I. 2) and Tertullian, *De pud.* 13 (CSEL 20. 244), and a number of letters addressed to St. Cyprian (e.g. Cyprian, *Ep.* 30. 8: CSEL 3. 2. 556) attest its use in Rome and North Africa; and at Alexandria, at any rate from 231, the bishop was regularly styled ὁ πάπας. There is a widespread notion that it belonged properly to the occupants of metropolitan sees, but this is not borne out by either the literary or the epigraphical evidence. In the West the custom of confining it to the bishop of Rome began to make headway in the fifth century. St. Augustine, although himself frequently addressed as *Papa* by his correspondents, supported this limitation, and his example was increasingly followed. Although the older usage lingered on (e.g. in 852 Eulogius, future archbishop of Toledo, addressed Wiliesindus of Pamplona as 'beatissime Papa': see PL 115. 845), it was virtually dead before the eighth century. In March, 1075, Gregory VII issued, as the eleventh of the famous twenty-seven propositions known as 'Dictatus Papae,' the claim that the title was the exclusive prerogative of the Holy See ('quod hoc unicum est nomen in mundo'). In fact, he was not so much creating a new situation as endorsing an existing one. On the whole question, see P. de Labriolle, 'Papa,' *Bulletin du Cange* 4 (1928) 65–75; H. Leclercq, 'Papa,' DACL 13. 1 (1937) 1097 ff.; H. Janssen, *Kultur und Sprache: zur Geschichte der alten Kirche im Spiegel der Sprachentwicklung von Tertullian bis Cyprian,* LCP 8 (1938) 93–96.

[2] The self-depreciation revealed here and in the rest of the paragraph was sincere, and was characteristic of Rufinus. Cf. *De ben. patr.* 1, praef. 3 (PL 21. 299) where he speaks of 'the poor level of my understanding,' and *ibid.* 2, praef. 1 and 2 (PL 21. 311 and 314), where he refers to 'my inexperience and my uncouth language,' and complains, 'I could not conceal my foolishness.' For another example, see *De ben. patr.* 2, *Ben.* 3 (PL 21. 336).

[3] This distinction has its roots in the New Testament. Cf. 1 Cor. 3. 1,

99

where St. Paul uses the phrase 'parvulis in Christo' taken up by Rufinus, and Heb. 5. 12–14, where the same contrast between *parvuli* and *perfecti* is found. Rufinus's point is that he expects his tract to be studied primarily by catechumens. At this period it was customary for catechumens to have the creed 'delivered' to them (this was the *traditio symboli*) at the beginning of the final week of their preparation, and to hear lectures on its contents daily between then and the solemn rite of 'giving back' the creed (the *redditio symboli*) immediately prior to their baptism. The eighteen *Catecheses* of St. Cyril of Jerusalem are samples of such lectures.

⁴ For examples of Rufinus's predecessors in the field, see Introd. 9 f.

⁵ Born at Ancyra, in Galatia, Photinus succeeded Eutherius as bishop of Sirmium, in Pannonia, in 343 or 344. A learned man and an attractive preacher, he was an extremist disciple of Marcellus of Ancyra: for his theology, see n. 247 below. He was condemned by the Easterns in 344 at the synod of Antioch which produced the *Ecthesis macrostichos* (see JNDK 279 f.), and by the Westerns in 345 and 347 at synods held at Milan. Despite successive excommunications, he managed to retain his see, and was only ejected after the second council of Sirmium (351). Permitted to return by Julian and again banished by Valentinian I, he eventually died in his own country in 376. Socrates (*Hist. eccl.* 2. 30: PG 67. 292) reports that he was the author of a work against all heresies in which he treated his own doctrines as the standard of orthodoxy; while St. Jerome (*De vir. ill.* 107: TU 14. 1. 49) attributes several books to him, including a *Contra gentes* and an *Ad Valentinum*. All have disappeared, and with them the essay on the creed referred to here.

⁶ Isa. 10. 22 f. Rufinus identifies the creed with the 'short word,' or concise summary, which he understands to be mentioned by the prophet. The original Hebrew may be translated: 'Destruction is decided upon, overflowing in righteous judgment: for an end, and that a decisive one, shall Yahweh make in the midst of the earth.' The Vulgate adheres fairly closely to this, rendering: 'Consummatio abbreviata inundabit iustitiam. Consummationem enim et abbreviationem Dominus Deus exercituum faciet in medio omnis terrae.' Rufinus, who never uses the Vulgate, is reproducing an Old Latin version based on the Septuagint, which at this point fails to understand the original. The text he quotes is supported by most of the Latin Fathers before him. It is noteworthy that his reading agrees exactly with that of Ambrosiaster: cf. *In Ep. ad Gal. prol.* (PL 17. 337).

⁷ The picturesque story of the compilation of the baptismal creed by the Apostles was already hallowed tradition when Rufinus wrote:

notice his words, 'tradunt maiores.' When and where it originated, we do not know: its first appearance is in another, slightly earlier North Italian document, the *Explanatio symboli ad initiandos* (PL 17. 1155 f.— see Introd. 10 and the attached n. 20), and in the sixth book of the *Apostolical Constitutions* (of Syrian origin, *ca.* 380). Niceta of Remesiana seems to allude to it (*De symbolo* 8: Burn 46); and it is also reflected in the title *Symbolum Apostolorum*, which first occurs in a letter (PL 16. 1125: it was probably drafted by St. Ambrose) sent in 390 by the synod of Milan to Pope Siricius. Later writers sometimes took up Rufinus's hint that each of the Twelve proposed a clause, and tried to identify their contributions: cf. esp. the pseudo-Augustinian sermon *De symbolo* (PL 39. 2189), and Priminius, *Scarapsus* 10 (Jecker 41). Taken literally, the story is inacceptable, although its thesis that the contents of the Church's creed have the authority of the Apostles behind them is solidly based. It is now agreed that creeds, in the sense of textually determined, officially sanctioned formulae, only began to emerge in the second century, and that even then there was no single, universally recognized text. The legend may be regarded as an uncritical elaboration of the conviction, widespread in the second century, that the 'rule of faith' was ultimately traceable to the Apostles. The 'rule' was an outline summary of Catholic doctrine used for catechetical purposes: it differed from the later creeds, in which its contents were absorbed, in having no fixed verbal form. St. Irenaeus, for example, explains (*Adv. haer.* 1. 2: Harvey 1. 90) that the 'rule' has been handed down from 'the Apostles and their disciples'; and Tertullian speaks (*Apol.* 47. 10: CSEL 69. 111) of 'the rule of truth which descends from Christ, transmitted through His companions.' Their claim was shared by all Catholic writers (see D. van den Eynde, *Les normes de l'enseignement chrétien* [Paris 1933]), and is justified by the New Testament emphasis on the Apostolic deposit of doctrine. On the whole question, see JNDK ch. 1.

[8] Rufinus is clearly wrong in ascribing the designation of the creed as *symbolum* to the Apostles. His idea that in Greek the word can mean 'joint compilation' is also mistaken: he is confusing σύμβολον with συμβολή, which does bear such a meaning, and allowing his philology to be influenced by his acceptance of the Apostolic compilation of the creed. Much more can be said in favour of his other suggestion, that *symbolum* means 'token' or 'sign': indeed this is the basic sense of the term. Many subsequent writers followed him in this interpretation, e.g. St. Maximus of Turin, *Hom.* 83 (PL 57. 433). Another plausible theory, supported by several contemporary writings (cf. Niceta, *De symbolo* 13: Burn 31; *Explanatio symboli ad initiandos*: PL 17. 1155; St. Augustine,

Sermons 212. 1 and 214. 12: PL 38. 1058 and 1072), links the word with the compact entered into between man and God at baptism. This agrees with the current use of *symbolum* as equivalent to 'legal bond,' 'covenant.' Attractive as these explanations are, however, neither of them lays bare the real significance of *symbolum* in this connection. Still less does the superficial modern view that the Church may have borrowed the term from the Mystery religions, in which cult emblems or formulae were sometimes called *symbola*: cf. A. Dieterich, *Eine Mithrasliturgie* (Leipzig 1923) 64. A serious objection to this is that the use of *symbolum* in reference to the creed seems to have originated in the West: the Greek-speaking churches were markedly slow to adopt it. The answer to our problem is supplied by a study of the earliest instances of the use of the term in connection with creeds: these occur in St. Cyprian's correspondence. In *Ep.* 69. 7 (CSEL 3. 2. 756) he discusses the claim that the heretic Novatian 'baptizes with the same *symbol*' as the Catholic Church; and in *Ep.* 75. 11 (CSEL 3. 2. 818) his friend Bishop Firmilian, describing the irregular baptism practised by a mad woman, admits that it did not lack 'the *symbol* of the Trinity.' The eighth canon of the Council of Arles of 314 (Mansi 3. 472) directs that heretics returning to the Church should be 'asked about the *symbol*.' The context in all these passages suggests that *symbolum* refers, not to a declaratory creed such as we are familiar with, but to the three credal questions (*interrogationes de fide*) which were addressed to candidates prior to baptism, coupled with the three immersions which followed the candidate's threefold assent. In the early centuries the asking of the questions, the candidate's answers, and the immersions constituted the decisive element in the rite. It seems probable, therefore, that the choice of *symbolum* was inspired by the idea that the triple questions, answers, and immersions symbolized the Triune God with whom the candidate was being united. By Rufinus's time this original significance had been lost sight of, partly because declaratory creeds, based on the old baptismal questions, had come to play a more prominent role, and the name *symbolum* had been transferred to them. See J. Brinktrine, *Theologische Quartalschrift* 102 (1921) 166 f.; O. Casel, *Jahrbuch für Liturgiewissenschaft* 2 (1922) 133 f.; H. J. Carpenter, JTS 43 (1942) 1–11; JNDK 52 ff.

[9] The references are to Rom. 16. 18 and Acts 19. 13.

[10] St. Cyril of Jerusalem, in his lectures on the creed, is profuse in his warnings that it must not be written down, but should be engraved in his hearers' memories: cf. *Procat.* 12; *Cat.* 5. 12, 6. 29. He himself was careful not to quote the actual text. This is the earliest evidence of that reticence about the creed which was fairly general throughout the

fourth century. St. Ambrose, for example, remarks: 'Beware of divulging imprudently the mystery of the Lord's Prayer and of the creed' (*De Cain et Abel* 1. 9. 37: CSEL 1. 370); while St. Jerome (*C. Ioann. Hieros.* 28: PL 23. 380) speaks of 'the symbol of our faith and hope, which has been handed down from the Apostles and is written, not on paper or with ink, but in the fleshly tables of the heart.' St. Augustine (*Serm.* 212. 2: PL 38. 1060) uses language almost identical with Rufinus's. This reticence was the result of the *disciplina arcani*, or rule of secrecy, which was operative from at least the third to the fifth century, and took the form of veiling the special mysteries of the Catholic religion (the sacraments, the Lord's Prayer, the creed) from the uninitiated. Rufinus attributes to it the further motive of preserving Apostolic doctrine unsullied. For an excellent early (end of second century?) example of a document written according to the *disciplina arcani*, see the celebrated Inscription of Abercius: cf. J. Quasten, *Patrology* 1 (Utrecht-Brussels 1950) 171 ff.

11 For the story of the Tower of Babel, see Gen. 11. 1–9. Verse 4 reads: *Let us make our name famous, before we be scattered abroad into all lands.* In the following sentence the mention of 'living stones' recalls 1 Pet. 2. 4 f.

12 The Latin reads 'in Deo Patre.' Although several MSS have 'in Deum Patrem,' the ablative is undoubtedly correct, both here and where the other divine Persons are mentioned. The distinction between the cases was at this period breaking down. From now onwards ablatives and accusatives were used indifferently, the exact significance of cases being lost sight of in the Middle Ages.

13 The letter of the synod of Milan (390) to Pope Siricius (*Ep.* 42. 5 of St. Ambrose: PL 16. 1125) agrees with this: 'credatur symbolo Apostolorum, quod ecclesia Romana intemeratum semper custodit et servat.' The implications of Rufinus's statement, taken in conjunction with what he elsewhere reveals of his purpose, are of immense importance for the history of creeds. He declares in effect (a) that he plans to expound the creed published by the Apostles, (b) that this is preserved in its authentic shape only at Rome, (c) that nevertheless, for reasons of personal piety, he proposes to base his commentary on the Aquileian text. It follows that he is bound to indicate at any rate the principal divergences between the Roman and Aquileian forms. Making this his starting-point, the seventeenth-century Archbishop J. Ussher (*De Romanae ecclesiae symbolo apostolico vetere . . . diatriba* [London 1647]) was able to make his brilliant reconstruction of the Old Roman Creed (known as R). He found his conjecture corroborated by the almost identical Greek creed which, more than sixty years before Rufinus

wrote, Marcellus of Ancyra inserted in the apologia which he addressed to Pope Julius I. The text of both creeds is printed in the Introd. 15 f. Ussher's inspired surmise has been abundantly confirmed in the twentieth century by the identification of the interrogatory creed in St. Hippolytus's *Apostolic Tradition* as a Roman baptismal confession of the first decades of the third century. The only important criticisms of the theory are those of F. J. Badcock—see *The History of the Creeds* (London 1930 and 1938)—but these do not hold water: cf. H. Lietzmann, *Zeitschrift für die Neutestamentliche Wissenschaft* 22 (1923) 257 f., and JNDK ch. 4. If the creed reconstructed from Rufinus and Marcellus is indeed the ancient baptismal confession of the Roman Church, it is clear that it lies behind all known baptismal creeds in the West: like the Aquileian formula, they are all variations of R. Rufinus, moreover, is right, if not in tracing R back to the Apostles, at any rate in his assumption that the creed of the Roman Church is uniquely ancient and had been preserved without significant alteration down to his time. We may add that the Roman Church did not adopt the enlarged, Gallicanized *textus receptus* of the Apostles' Creed until at earliest the ninth century, and possibly much later. See Introd. 16 f. and JNDK chs. 4 and 13.

¹⁴ The rite referred to is the *redditio symboli*, which marked the conclusion of the catechumen's preparation and the beginning of the baptism proper: see n. 3 above. St. Augustine confirms (*Conf.* 8. 2. 5: CSEL 33. 173) that as carried out at Rome the ceremony was peculiarly solemn and public: it took place, he says, 'de loco eminentiore in conspectu populi fidelis.'

¹⁵ Rufinus's suggestion is to a certain extent true. Much of the material, for example, embodied in the present Nicene Creed owes (cf. especially 'genitum, non factum, consubstantialem Patri') its presence there to the desire to define the faith more strictly against heresy. On the other hand, the additional clauses which appear in the provincial variants of R were very rarely inserted for polemical reasons. Most of them (e.g. 'sanctorum communionem') give expression to ideas which churchmen had come to prize for their own sake.

¹⁶ Like many other contemporaries who were sons of religious mothers (St. Augustine, St. Basil, St. Gregory Nazianzen, St. John Chrysostom), Rufinus waited until early manhood before being baptized. His formal reception into the Church took place in 369 or 370, when he was 24 or 25: cf. his statement in *Apol. in Hier.* 1. 4 (PL 21. 543). In *Ad Anast.* 4 (PL 21. 625) he repeats that he received his baptism 'in Aquileiensi ecclesia.'

¹⁷ Heb. 11. 6. Rufinus quotes it inexactly, interpolating 'first of all,'

and changing 'them that seek Him' in the original to 'them that believe in Him.'

[18] Isa. 7. 9. The Vulgate, adhering closely to the Hebrew, reads: 'Nisi credideritis, non permanebitis.' Rufinus's text 'non intelligetis' translates the Septuagint, and is supported by most of the Latin fathers. Cf. Ambrosiaster, *De interp. Iob et David* I. 29 (PL 14. 809); St. Augustine, *Ep.* 120. 3 (CSEL 34. 706), etc.

[19] In this passage Rufinus, like other Christian apologists, tries to show that faith is not an isolated decision, alien to man's normal life and only instanced in his acceptance of revelation: it is an element in his conduct of his everyday affairs. He echoes St. Cyril of Jerusalem, who cites (*Cat.* 5. 3) the examples of marriage, farming, seafaring, and business generally. St. Augustine defines faith in this sense as 'cum assensione cogitare' (*De praed. sanct.* 5: PL 44. 962 f.). He, too, dwells on its necessity for the ordinary routine of life: cf. *De util. cred.* 26 (CSEL 25. 34); *De civ. Dei* 11. 3 (CSEL 40. 1. 514).

[20] From the first the Church's suspicion of mere rationalism (cf. 1 Cor. 1. 20 f.; Col. 2. 8) and insistence on faith had been a stumbling block to the educated pagan world. Cf. Celsus's caricature (in Origen, *C. Cels.* 1. 9: GCS 1. 61=Chadwick 12): 'Some refuse to give or hear reason about their faith, but stick to their principle, "Ask no questions, just believe (μὴ ἐξέταζε, ἀλλὰ πίστευσον)," and "Thy faith shall save thee."' Cf. also *C. Cels.* 3. 75 (GCS 1. 267=Chadwick 178 f.). Eusebius, probably with Porphyry in mind (*Praep. Ev.* 1. 1: PG 21. 25 ff.), reproduces the complaint that Christians 'confirm their opinions by an unreasoning faith and an assent without examination': they urge their converts 'to adhere to faith alone,' and are called believers 'because of their uncritical and untested faith.' The Apostate Julian (in Gregory Naz., *Or.* 4. 102: PG 35. 636 f.) took up what had become a stock charge against the Church: 'Ours are reasoned arguments,' he said, 'all your wisdom can be summed up in the command, "Believe!"' There is an important discussion of this aspect of the anti-Christian pagan polemic in R. Walzer's *Galen on Jews and Christians* (Oxford 1949) 48 ff. A good example of a Christian offering a handle to such attacks is Consentius, whom St. Augustine in *Ep.* 120 (CSEL 34. 704 ff.) gently recalls to a proper estimation of the place of reason in relation to faith.

[21] Compare the creeds of Caesarea, Jerusalem, etc.: also the Nicene and Nicaeo-Constantinopolitan creeds. Rufinus has laid his finger on one of the main differences between Eastern and Western creeds. It is so striking that scholars were formerly tempted to infer, particularly in view of the presence of 'one God the Father' in the versions of the 'rule of faith' recorded by St. Irenaeus and Tertullian, that 'one' must

A.C.W.R.—8

originally have stood in the first article of R, but was deliberately excised at the time of the Monarchian controversy as liable to offer a foothold to Sabellianism. But it is incredible that so characteristic an article of the faith, granted it once had a place in the creed, could ever have been jettisoned because of its supposed encouragement of heresy. As a matter of fact, there is plenty of second-century Roman creed material (e.g. in St. Justin's writings) which testifies to the existence of affirmations of belief in God without the epithet 'one' long before Sabellianism became a menace. It must be regarded as a typically Roman trait.

²² This is broadly true, but there are exceptions: e.g. the creeds of the *Apostolical Constitutions* (7. 41: Funk 1. 444 ff.), and of Antioch (cf. Cassian, *C. Nest.* 6. 3. 2: CSEL 17. 327) lack 'one' before 'Jesus Christ.'

²³ He refers to the Pauline formula (1 Cor. 8. 6): *There is but one God, the Father, of whom are all things, and we unto him; and one Lord Jesus Christ, by whom are all things, and we by Him.* It is clear that this text influenced the structure and wording of many Eastern creeds. The pioneer of modern credal research, H. Lietzmann, probably went too far when he argued (cf. *Geschichte der alten Kirche* [Berlin-Leipzig 1936] 2. 107 f.) that all creeds, Western as well as Eastern, were founded on it.

²⁴ This argument for the reciprocal necessitation of the terms 'father' and 'son' derives ultimately from Aristotle (see *Categories* 7 for his discussion of 'the relative'). It became classic among orthodox theologians. A long time before Rufinus, Tertullian had pointed out (*Adv. Prax.* 10: Evans 98): 'A father, to be father, must necessarily have a son; and a son, to be a son, a father.' Cf. Dionysius of Alexandria (in St. Athanasius, *De sent. Dion.* 17: PG 25. 504): 'I mention the Father, and, before introducing the Son, I have already mentioned Him in the Father. I introduce the Son; but even if I have not already mentioned the Father, He has already been understood in the Son.' St. Athanasius fully exploited the line of thought, as in *C. Ar.* 3. 6 (PG 26. 333): 'No one could speak of the Father if the Son did not exist. . . . He who names the Father indicates the existence of the Son at the same time as the Father.'

²⁵ The ineffable nature of the Son's eternal generation, transcending all analogy with human birth processes, was a commonplace of fourth-century orthodoxy. Cf., e.g. St. Athanasius, *De decret. Nic. syn.* 11 f. (PG 25. 441 ff.); St. Basil, *Adv. Eunom.* 2. 6 ff. (PG 29. 581 ff.). St. Gregory of Nazianzus points out (*Or. theol.* 3. 8: PG 36. 84) that men do not understand their own birth, and concludes: 'So let God's genera-

tion be adored in silence. It is a privilege to know that He (i.e. the Son) has been born. But how, we shall grant not even angels to know, much less you to understand.' This refusal to analyse the mystery was in deliberate reaction to the Arian habit of pressing the analogy of human birth to render their own theories of the Son's status and nature more plausible. Notice that St. Cyril of Jerusalem (*Cat.* 11. 11–13) insists at greater length, in language which Rufinus echoes, on the incomprehensibility of the divine generation.

[26] In this important passage Rufinus comes near to suggesting that the mind and its processes present an analogy to the divine Trinity: St. Augustine was contemporaneously working this out in his *De trinitate*. For Rufinus, however, the relation between the mind and its concepts, or the mind and memory, at most illustrates the unity in difference of Father and Son, and the immateriality of the divine generation. Almost at once he passes to the familiar analogies handed down in the Greek patristic tradition: the river and its source, the light and its brightness.

[27] Matt. 17. 5.

[28] The quotations are from John 14. 9, 10. 30, and 16. 28. The Vulgate text of the last-mentioned reads: 'exivi a Patre (cf. 13. 3: "A Deo exivit") et veni in mundum.'

[29] The point Rufinus is seeking to make (his words are 'non . . . unum numero dici, sed universitate') is that number is inapplicable to God: not being one of a class, as created things are, He transcends the category of number. Cf. St. Thomas, *Summa theol.* I q. 11, art. 3. His analogy of the sun is scarcely apt, for, though there is in fact only one sun, a second or third sun is in principle conceivable; whereas no second God is conceivable. Evagrius Ponticus, in a letter ascribed to St. Basil (*Ep.* 8. 2: PG 32. 248 f.), supplies a useful commentary, although he treats the problem of the applicability of number to the Godhead from a rather different angle: 'Let this be our answer to those who charge us with tritheism: we confess God as one in nature, not numerically one. Whatever is defined as numerically one is not really one or simple in nature: but all agree that God is simple and uncompounded by nature. Therefore God is not numerically one. . . . We abolish number from His blessed and intelligible nature. Number belongs to quantity, and quantity is bound up with bodily nature.' For a full discussion see R. Arnou's article, 'Unité numérique et unité de nature chez les Pères, après le concile de Nicée,' in *Gregorianum* 15 (1934) 242 ff.

[30] Rufinus's interpretation reproduces what was at any rate the chief strain in the original meaning of 'omnipotens' in the creed: the Greek

was παντοκράτωρ. We may compare St. Irenaeus's argument against the graded hierarchy of divine beings postulated by the Gnostics (*Adv. haer.* 2. 1. 5.: Harvey 1. 253 f.): 'Either there must be one God who contains all things and has made every created being according to His will; or else there must be many indeterminate creators or gods. . . . But not one of them will be God. For each of them will be defective in comparison of the rest, and the name of "Almighty" will come to nought.' St. Theophilus of Antioch explains that God is called almighty 'because He rules and compasses all things' (*Ad Autol.* 1. 4: Otto 8. 14). Rufinus's master, St. Cyril of Jerusalem, remarks: '"Almighty" is the name for Him who rules all things, who holds sway over all things' (*Cat.* 8. 3). The alternative meaning, 'able to do all things,' existed side by side with this, and eventually came to the fore: cf. Origen, *C. Cels.* 3. 70 (GCS 1. 262 = Chadwick 175); St. Augustine, *Serm.* 213. 1; 214. 4 (PL 38. 1060 f. and 1067 f.).

³¹ Col. 1. 16. Instead of Rufinus's text ('per ipsum creata sunt omnia'), the Vulgate reads 'in ipso condita sunt universa in caelis et in terra.' Rufinus's 'per ipsum' is without parallel: he has doubtless altered the original so as to make it fit in with his exposition. The use of 'creata' and 'condita' agrees with the general Old Latin tradition.

³² Heb. 1. 2. Rufinus quotes inexactly: the two clauses are in the inverse order in the original.

³³ Apoc. 4. 8. The Vulgate, which accurately reproduces the Greek, reads 'dicentia' (Rufinus: 'dicentes'), and 'dominus deus omnipotens' (Rufinus: 'dominus deus sabaoth'), and has no final 'omnipotens.'

³⁴ What Rufinus says is interestingly confirmed by a passage of the *Explanatio symboli ad initiandos* (PL 17. 1157), which states: 'When the Patripassians emerged, the Catholics deemed it suitable to add "invisible" and "impassible" in this clause, implying thereby that it was the Son of God who was visible and passible. If He was visible in the flesh, it was His flesh, and not His divinity, which was visible.' The author goes on to criticize the insertion of such an addition, however well-intentioned, to 'what the Apostles prescribed,' pointing out that the Arians had been able to twist the words to their advantage.

³⁵ Patripassianism was the Western name for the Modalist version of Monarchianism. In their dread of ditheism, the Patripassians so strongly emphasized the unity of God that the distinction between Father and Son disappeared: hence He who in the Person of Jesus Christ was born, suffered, died, and rose again was identical with the Father. Noetus expounded ideas like these in Asia Minor in the closing decades of the second century, and was condemned at Smyrna: for his views, see St. Hippolytus, *C. Noet.*, *passim* (PG 10. 804 ff.); St. Epiphanius,

Haer. 57 (GCS 31. 343 ff.). Their most notable representative at Rome was Praxeas, whose activity coincided with the pontificate of Victor I (189–98): for his date, see G. La Piana, *Harvard Theol. Rev.* 18 (1925) 245 n. 48. In his teaching he took pains to distinguish a duality in Jesus Christ, speaking of the man Jesus as being properly 'the Son,' while 'Christ,' the divine element, was the Father: hence the formula, 'Filius sic quidem patitur, Pater vero compatitur': see Tertullian, *Adv. Prax.*, *passim*, but esp. 27 and 29 (Evans 123–25, 127 f.). Sabellius, who came upon the scene somewhat later, in the reign of Pope Zephyrinus (198–217), is reported (St. Basil, *Ep.* 207. 1 [PG 32. 760]) to have been a Libyan, a supposition which accords well with the diffusion of his doctrine in the Libyan Pentapolis in the days of Pope Dionysius the Great (247/8–64/5). His theory was that the Persons of the Trinity, so far from being of the essence of the Godhead, are only names for the three successive manifestations which the divine Monad has assumed in His relation to the created order. St. Hippolytus discusses his ideas in *Ref. omn. haer.* 9. 11 f. (GCS. 26. 245 ff.).

[36] Bar. 3. 36–38. Rufinus's Latin text differs from the Vulgate, but not so as to alter the sense. Both are samples of the Old Latin, since St. Jerome did not regard Baruch as canonical (cf. *Prol. in lib. Ierem*: PL 28. 848) and so did not retouch it. His attitude was singular: almost every Christian writer of importance treated it as Scripture, and its claims were finally vindicated at the Council of Trent. The passage under discussion was extremely popular in the early Church, being cited by at least thirty authors in the first five centuries. St. Hippolytus reports (*C. Noet.* 2: PG 10. 805) that the Patripassians appealed to it as proving that He who appeared on earth was God the Father. Apart from this isolated interpretation, the Fathers generally took it as an inspired prophecy of the Messiah. The Greek original of v. 38 (ὤφθη καὶ τοῖς ἀνθρώποις συνανεστράφη) makes it clear that Wisdom, which is the theme of the whole passage and stands for the Second Person of the Godhead, is the subject of both verbs. By altering them to the masculine ('visus est' . . . 'conversatus est'), the Latin makes ambiguity possible, but the intention was to bring out all the more emphatically that the personal Messiah was the logical subject. The verse has sometimes been suspected of being a Christian gloss (see O. C. Whitehouse, in Charles, *Apocrypha and Pseudepigrapha of the O.T.* 591 n.), but on insufficient grounds.

[37] We notice that the Aquileian creed, like the Old Roman creed and the baptismal questionnaire in St. Hippolytus's *Apostolic Tradition*, retains the primitive order 'Christ Jesus.' This reflects a time when 'Christ' was still felt to be a title, meaning 'Messiah' or 'the Anointed.'

[38] The name 'Jesus' is a Greek transcript of the Hebrew 'Jeshua' or 'Joshua,' meaning 'Jehovah is salvation.' Cf. Matt. 1. 21: *Thou shalt call His name JESUS. For He shall save His people from their sins.* Philo (*De mut. nom.* 1. 597) gives exactly the same explanation. Eusebius, in *Dem. Ev.* 4. 17. 23 (GCS 23. 199 f.), remarks that 'Jesus' means 'salvation of God.' St. Cyril of Jerusalem, while fancifully deriving the Greek 'Iησοῦς from ἰᾶσθαι (='to heal'), explains that in Hebrew it signifies 'saviour.'

[39] The Greek ὁ Χριστός (from χρίω='anoint') was the regular Septuagint translation of the Hebrew Messiah, which also means 'anointed.'

[40] For the change of Osee's name to Josue (Jesus), see Num. 12. 8. Early Christian thought regarded Josue as a type of Our Lord, and saw significance in the change. Cf. *Epistle of St. Barnabas* 12. 8–10 (Funk-Bihlmeyer 26=ACW 6.55 f.); St. Justin, *Dial.* 75, 113, 132 (Archambault 2. 4; 182; 272); St. Irenaeus, *Epideixis* 27 (Robinson 94 ff.= ACW 16. 65); Tertullian, *Adv. Marc.* 3. 16 (CSEL 47. 402 f.).

[41] St Cyril also connects 'Christus' with Our Lord's priestly status: cf. *Cat.* 10. 4, 10. 11, 10. 14. For the unction of the high priest and other priests, see Exod. 30. 25–32; Lev. 8. 12; etc. For the unction of kings, see 1 Kings 9. 16, 10. 1, 15. 1 (anointing of Saul by Samuel); *ibid.* 16. 3 and 12 f. (anointing of David by Samuel). St. Augustine (*De trin.* 15. 46: PL 42. 1093 f.) traced our Lord's anointing with the Holy Spirit back to His conception in the womb. The more general tradition was that it took place at His baptism, when (Matt. 3. 16) the Holy Spirit descended upon Him: cf. St. Hilary, *De trin.* 11. 18 (PL 10. 412); St. Athanasius, *C. Ar.* 1. 47 (PG 26. 108 f.); St. Jerome, *In Is.* 17. 61 (PL 24. 599).

[42] Acts 10. 38. Rufinus adds 'misso de coelis.'

[43] Isa. 61. 1. The Vulgate reads 'Spiritus Domini super me, eo quod unxerit Dominus me: ad annunciandum mansuetis misit me,' where Rufinus has 'Spiritus Domini super me: propter quod unxit me, evangelizare misit me pauperibus.' Rufinus's text was one widely used in the West: cf. St. Ambrose, *De Sp. Sancto* 3. 1 (PL 16. 777).

[44] Rufinus echoes Heb. 5. 6, which quotes Ps. 109. 4: 'Thou art a priest forever according to the order of Melchisedech.' St. Cyril also appealed to the text when speaking of our Lord's priesthood: *Cat.* 10. 11, 10. 14.

[45] The Arians, exploiting the analogy of human generation, urged that, if Christ was truly God's Son, the divine substance must have suffered division or separation. The Catholic rejoinder was that the divine substance was spiritual, not material, and therefore the analogy

could not be pressed. St. Athanasius deals fully with the objection in
De decret. Nic. syn. 11 (PG 25. 441 ff.), showing that, because the Godhead is spiritual and therefore simple, the Father can beget the Son
without that division or plurality resulting which are inevitable in
human generation. Cf. St. Cyril, *Cat.* 7. 5.

⁴⁶ Cf. Rom. 16. 27 (*God, the only wise*) and 1 Cor. 1. 24 (*Christ, the
power of God and the wisdom of God*).

⁴⁷ 1 Cor. 11. 3. The Vulgate reads: 'Caput vero Christi Deus.' The
addition of 'est,' which is found in Rufinus, was also a feature of the
text St. Ambrose knew: cf. *Exp. Ev. Luc.* 6.14, 7. 32 (PL 15. 1672,
1708). He also, it would seem, omits 'vero,' as does Rufinus. St. Cyril
of Jerusalem appeals to the same text when discussing the Son's generation from the Father and arguing that there are not two unoriginate
principles, but only one: cf. *Cat.* 11. 14. There is much uncertainty as to
the true text of the closing lines of this chapter: see the note *ad loc.* in
Migne. The confusion is doubtless the result of scribal glosses: the
intricate theology of the passage seemed puzzling and invited attempts
at clarification.

⁴⁸ We may compare St. Cyril, *Cat.* 11. 7: 'And when you hear of
God begetting, sink not down in thought to bodily things, nor think of
a corruptible generation, lest you be guilty of impiety. "God is a
spirit": His generation is spiritual. For bodies beget bodies.' Again,
ibid. 11. 8: 'Think not, therefore, that this generation is human, nor as
Abraham begot Isaac.' The orthodox repeatedly emphasized the utter
unlikeness of the generation of the Son of God to human generation,
pointing to the immateriality of the divine nature. Cf. St. Athanasius's
complaint against the Arians, 'who, in order that they may not confess
the Son to be the Father's image, think of the Father Himself in bodily
and earthly terms' (*C. Ar.* 1. 21: PG 26. 56). The illustrations which
follow, of the human word and the brightness of light, were classic in
Catholic thought: see St. Athanasius, *C. Ar.* 2. 33 f. (PG 26. 217 ff.).
They are intended to show that there are examples of generations
which do not involve the division of the parent's substance, or the
separation of the offspring from it.

⁴⁹ For objections of this sort, see St. Athanasius, *C. Ar.* 2. 34 (PG
26. 220): 'For the word of men, composed as it is of syllables, has hardly
indicated the speaker's will when it ceases and disappears.' St. Cyril
(*Cat.* 11. 10) admits their force in language which anticipates Rufinus:
'The Father did not beget the Son as among men the mind begets its
word. For the mind exists in us as a substance; but the word, once
spoken, is dispersed into the air and comes to an end.'

⁵⁰ For a similar argument that illustrations are to be taken as

analogies, not direct likenesses, cf. St. Athanasius, *C. Ar.* 3. 22 f. (PG 26. 369 ff.). St. Augustine makes the same point effectively with reference to the story of the sons of Noe in *De civ. Dei* 16. 2. 3 (CSEL 40. 2. 127): 'Non sane omnia quae gesta narrantur aliquid etiam significare putanda sunt; sed propter illa quae aliquid significant etiam ea quae nihil significant attexuntur.' In his discussion of the Gospel parables Rufinus proves that the Fathers were not always open to the charge, brought against them by modern critics—cf. e.g. C. H. Dodd, *The Parables of the Kingdom* (London 1936) 11—of turning them into allegories. St. John Chrysostom was another who several times protested against this tendency: cf. e.g. *In Matt. hom.* 64 (PG 58. 613): 'We ought not to investigate the details of the parables literally, but we should first discover the main point for the sake of which they were put together (τὸν σκοπὸν μαθόντας δι᾽ ὃν συνετέθη), and then concentrate on this and not bother about the rest.'

⁵¹ Matt. 13. 33. The Vulgate has 'acceptum,' which Rufinus probably omits by oversight. It also reads 'mulier abscondit in farinae satis tribus' for his Old Latin 'abscondit mulier in farinae mensuris tribus.'

⁵² *Ibid.* 13. 47. The Vulgate reads 'sagenae missae in mare et ex omni genere piscium congreganti' where Rufinus, following the Old Latin, has 'reti misso in mare, quod ex omni genere piscium abstrahit.'

⁵³ In harmony with R and practically all Western creeds, the Aquileian creed has 'unicum.' The word represents the Greek μονογενής, which is used in the New Testament only by St. Luke (7. 12, 8. 42, 9. 38), St. John (1. 14, 1. 18, 3. 16, 3. 18, 1 John 4. 9), and St. Paul in Hebrews (11. 17). Its ordinary meaning is clearly brought out in Luke 7. 12, where Our Lord raises up 'the only son' of the widow of Naim. As indicating the peculiar relationship of Jesus to God the Father, it is confined to the Johannine writings, where it stresses His uniqueness alike in His Sonship, in His intimacy with His Father, and in His consequent knowledge of Him. Cf. F. Büchsel, TWNT 4 (1942) s. v. 747–50. Its occurrence in second-century Christian writings prior to St. Irenaeus is rare. It is possible that orthodox churchmen began claiming it as a title of Our Lord about his time because the Valentinian Gnostics were tending to monopolize it as a designation for their aeon Nous, making a sharp distinction between Monogenes and the historical Jesus. See St. Irenaeus, *Adv. haer.* 3. 16. (Harvey 2. 81 f.); also JNDK 141 ff.

⁵⁴ St. Ambrose also referred 'only' to 'Lord' as well as to 'Son': cf. *Explan. symb. ad init.* (PL 17. 1157): 'Sic dicite, *Filium eius unicum.* Non unicus Dominus? Unus Deus est, unus et Dominus. Sed ne

calumnientur et dicant, quia una persona est: dicamus Filium etiam unicum Dominum nostrum.'

⁵⁵ Cf. St. Cyril, *Cat.* 11. 2: 'When you hear of the Son, do not suppose Him an adoptive Son, but a Son by nature (φυσικὸν υἱόν), an only-begotten Son who has no brother'; and *ibid.* 11. 7: 'He is thus the Son of God by nature, and not by adoption (φύσει καὶ οὐ θέσει).'

⁵⁶ 1 Cor. 8. 6.

⁵⁷ The Old Roman creed probably had 'who was born from (*de*—Gk. ἐκ) the Holy Spirit and the Virgin Mary': so at any rate the Greek version cited by Marcellus of Ancyra (in St. Epiphanius, *Haer.* 72. 3: GCS 37. 258) and the Latin text of Codex Laud. Gr. 35 of the Bodleian Library suggest. The more precise description, '*by* the Holy Spirit *from* the Virgin Mary,' appears in the baptismal questionnaire in St. Hippolytus's *Apostolic Tradition*, in the creed of Milan discoverable from *Explan. symb. ad init.* (PL 17. 1156), and in the creeds of Hippo and Carthage. The fuller text of the present Apostles' Creed, 'qui conceptus est de Spiritu sancto, natus ex Maria Virgine,' is first evidenced in the formulary drafted, according to St. Jerome (*Dial. c. Lucif.* 7: PL 23. 170 f.), by the orthodox party at Rimini in 359 and attributed to one of its leading members, Phoebadius of Agen. It featured in Gallican formularies of the sixth century, e.g. at Riez and Arles. See JNDK 172 ff. and 376 ff.

⁵⁸ Isa. 7. 14. Actually, the only direct quotation of the text in the Gospels is Matt. 1. 23: Luke 1. 31 clearly echoes it.

⁵⁹ Like his master Origen, Rufinus followed the Alexandrine school of Scriptural exegesis, with its bias towards allegorical interpretation. We shall come across many examples of this in the remainder of the treatise. Similar tendencies can be observed in other Latin writers of the fourth century, such as St. Hilary and St. Ambrose.

⁶⁰ Ezech. 44. 2. As usual, Rufinus cites the Old Latin, which follows the Septuagint. The Vulgate has: 'Porta haec clausa erit; non aperietur, et vir non transibit per eam, quoniam Dominus Deus Israel ingressus est per eam; eritque clausa principi.' The original reference is to the restored Temple of Jerusalem which Ezechiel saw in his vision: once 'the majesty of the Lord' has entered it (cf. perfect tense, 'ingressus est,' in the Vulgate) by the Eastern gate (cf. 43. 4), the gate will be shut.

The application of Ezechiel's 'porta clausa' to the Blessed Virgin was to become popular in the Eastern and the Western Church. St. Jerome, although himself explaining the passage in the light of Matt. 23. 13 and Luke 11. 52, commends those who refer the words to the Virgin, 'quae et ante partum et post partum virgo permansit' (*Comm. in Ezech.* 13. 44: PL 25. 449). St. Ambrose wrote (*Ep.* 42. 6: PL 16. 1126):

'Quae autem est illa porta sanctuarii, porta illa exterior ad Orientem, quae manet clausa? . . . Nonne haec porta Maria est, per quam in hunc mundum Redemptor intravit?' Cf. also the Christmas hymn of St. John Damascene in PG 96. 824, and the office of Lauds in *Breviarium Ambrosianum* for 15 Aug. and 8 Sept. A fairly full list of patristic references is given by A. Grohmann, *Äthiopische Marienhymnen: Abhand. der sächs. Akad. der Wiss.*, Phil.—hist. Kl. 33 (1919) 184 f.

[61] In agreement with St. Jerome in the text cited above, and with the patristic tradition generally, Rufinus supports the perpetual virginity, *post partum* as well as *in partu*, of Our Lady. Cf. St. Augustine's formula (*De cat. rud.* 40: PL 40. 339), 'virgo concipiens, virgo pariens, virgo moriens,' and his frequent use of the formula, 'virgo concepit, virgo peperit, virgo permansit' (e.g. *Serm.* 51. 18; 190. 2; 196. 1: PL 38. 343; 1008; 1019). The dogma of the perpetual virginity came into particular prominence in the closing decades of the fourth century. While the patristic teaching during the first three centuries had been firm on the point—see E. Dublanchy, 'Marie IV: enseignement traditionnel,' DTC 9. 2 (1927) 2369–73; also J. C. Plumpe, *Theol. Stud.* 9 (1948) 567–77—the emergence of heretical views about 390 rendered a more emphatic assertion of the truth desirable. Helvidius, for example, maintained that the Virgin had borne children to St. Joseph subsequently to the birth of Our Lord; and St. Jerome wrote a spirited rejoinder to him in his *De perpet. virg. B. Mar. adv. Helvid.* (PL 23. 183 ff.). Another heretic, Bonosus, bishop of Sardica, sponsored similar views, and was condemned at the synod of Capua in 391: cf. the letter of Pope Siricius, dated about 392, printed in PL 13. 1176–78. The official mind of the Church received expression at the synod of Milan held in 390, which affirmed the absolute virginity of Mary both in conceiving and in giving birth to the Saviour, and throughout the remainder of her life: see PL 16. 1125 f.

[62] Luke 1. 31. Rufinus seems to be quoting from memory and confusing this passage with Matt. 1. 21, where the angel addresses St. Joseph and adds: *For He shall save His people from their sins.* In the Lucan passage the angel addresses Mary in the words: 'He shall be great, and shall be called the Son of the Most High,' etc. Rufinus's Latin text differs in detail from the Vulgate, giving 'hic enim' for 'ipse enim' and 'peccatis suis' for 'peccatis eorum.'

[63] *Ibid.* 1. 34 and 35. Rufinus differs from the Vulgate in giving 'veniet super te' for 'superveniet in te' and 'et ideo' for 'ideoque': he also inserts 'ex te' after 'nascetur.'

[64] Rufinus's exegesis is most interesting: for the history of the interpretation of Luke 1. 34 ff., see O. Bardenhewer, *Mariä Verkündigung.*

Ein Kommentar zu Lukas 1, 26–28, in *Bibl. Studien* 10. 5 (Freiburg i. Br.
1905) 132. The prevailing fashion until the fourth century was to
understand 'Holy Spirit' and 'Power of the Most High' as referring
to the Logos: the theory was that He, as it were, incarnated Himself
in the Virgin's womb. Cf. St. Justin, *Apol.* 1. 33 (Rauschen 53 f.);
Dial. 105 (Archambault 2. 144). As the doctrine of the Holy Spirit
became more clearly defined, the tendency was to equate 'Power of
the Most High' (cf. 1 Cor. 1. 24) with the eternal Son and 'Holy
Spirit' with the third Person of the Trinity. This is the view adopted
by Rufinus here, and it continued to be held throughout the Middle
Ages, finding such important exponents as St. John Damascene (*De
fid. orth.* 3. 2: PG 94. 985) and St. Thomas Aquinas (*Summa theol.* 3,
8. 32, art. 1. 1). In the Evangelist's mind, however, 'Holy Spirit' and
'Power of the Most High' undoubtedly stood for the same divine
reality, viz. the third Person of the Godhead.

   [65] For pagan disbelief of the Lord's virginal conception, see Origen,
C. Cels. 1. 37, 6. 73 (GCS 2. 88 f., 3. 142 f.=Chadwick 36, 286 f.).
In the former passage Origen anticipates Rufinus's line of reasoning,
pointing out (a) that there are examples of parthenogenesis even in the
animal kingdom (e.g. among vultures), and (b) that Greek history (e.g.
Plato's alleged birth from Perictione by Apollo: see Diogenes
Laertius 3. 2) and mythology (cf. the stories of Danae, Melanippe, etc.)
abound in similar tales. St. Cyril (*Cat.* 12. 27) has a brief paragraph out-
lining an *argumentum ad hominem* closely resembling that of Rufinus.

   [66] The legend of the phoenix had many forms and underwent considerable development. Among our main sources of information
about it are Herodotus 2. 73; Tacitus, *Ann.* 6. 28; Pliny, *Nat. hist.*
10. 2; St. Clement of Rome, *Ad Cor.* 25 (Funk-Bihlmeyer 49; cf.
ACW 1. 109 n. 79). According to the *Physiologus*, or *Bestiary*, which
was widely studied in the Middle Ages, the mythical bird was a native
of India and had a life-span of 500 years. On attaining this age, it made
for Heliopolis, in Egypt, with its wings laden with frankincense and
spices, and there burned itself on the altar of sacrifice. On the following
day the priest discovered in its ashes a worm, with wings sprouting
from it: this grew into a new phoenix, and on the third day flew back
to its native land. Among pagans the phoenix was a symbol of eternity:
cf. its use by Martial (*Epig.* 5. 7) and on imperial coins (see Cohen
2. 435 no. 129) to illustrate the 'aeternitas Romae.' On the question,
see A. Rusch, 'Phoinix,' in Pauly-Wissowa-Kroll, *Realenzyclopädie*
20. 1 (1941) 422. Among Christians the symbolism of the phoenix had an
enormous vogue: usually it suggested to them the idea of resurrection.
Cf. Tertullian, *De carn. resurr.* 13 (CSEL 47. 42); St. Cyril, *Cat.* 18. 8.

A second strand of tradition, however, stressed the absence of any carnal intercourse in the rebirth of the phoenix from its own ashes: cf. Lactantius (?), *De ave phoenice* 164 (CSEL 27. 146), ('Felix, quae Veneris foedera nulla colit'), and St. Zeno of Verona, *Tract.* 16. 9 (PL 11. 381) ('ipsa est sibi uterque sexus . . . non ex coitu nascitur'). This is the symbolism to which Rufinus here appeals. For numismatic, artistic, and epigraphical representations of the phoenix, see H. Leclercq, 'Phénix,' DACL 14. 1 (1939) 687—91.

[67] This erroneous theory was widely held in antiquity: it could boast the support of Aristotle (*Hist. anim.* 5. 21) and Pliny (*Nat. hist.* 11. 16). Virgil made it authoritative in literature when he wrote (*Georg.* 4. 198 ff.):

quod neque concubitu indulgent, nec corpora segnes
in Venerem solvunt, aut fetus nixibus edunt;
verum ipsae e foliis natos et suavibus herbis
ore legunt.

[68] Minerva was the Italian goddess of handicrafts: she was regularly identified with the Greek Athene. A leading feature of the latter's myth was the story of her birth from the head of Zeus. It was already fully developed by the time Pindar (518–438 B.C.) wrote *Ol.* 7. 35. The head of Zeus was supposed to have been split with an axe by Hephaestus, or some other personage, and the goddess to have sprung forth, fully armed and uttering her war cry. St. Cyril (*Cat.* 12. 27) cites the same example.

[69] Liber was the Italian god of fertility, and especially of wine. He was understood to be identical with the Greek Dionysus. According to the legend, the latter was born at Thebes, the son of Zeus, the fertilizing rain-god, and Semele, personifying the earth. Zeus revealed himself to Semele, at her own earnest but ill-judged request, when she was pregnant, and she was at once consumed by the fire of his thunderbolts. Zeus then seized the unborn child, and thrust him into his own thigh, from which he was born in due course. Cf. Euripides, *Bacch.* 295; Ovid, *Fast.* 3. 715 f. This was also one of St. Cyril's illustrations in *Cat.* 12. 27.

[70] The true meaning of the name of Aphrodite, the Greek goddess of love, beauty, and fertility, is uncertain. Legend had it that she was born from the foam of the sea, at Cythera, and from Hesiod (*Theog.* 188–206) onwards the Greeks liked to derive her name from ἀφρός (='foam'). Cf. Plato, *Crat.* 406c.

[71] Castor and Pollux, the Dioscuri, were fabled to be sons of Zeus and Leda (*Hymn. Hom.* 33. 1 ff.), and brothers of Helen (Homer, *Il.* 3. 237 ff.). The legend that they were both born from an egg finds its first mention in Horace, *Serm.* 2. 1. 26.

⁷² The Myrmidons were, in Greek mythology, an Achaean race inhabiting Phtiotis, in Thessaly. In Homer (*Il.* 1. 180, 2. 683 ff., etc.) they appear as Achilles's followers. They seem to have been immigrants from Aegina, where, according to the tradition, the ants (μύρμηκες) had been transformed by Zeus into men in the time of King Aeacus because the whole population had died of plague. See Strabo, *Geog.* 8. 375, 9. 433.

⁷³ For this story, see Ovid, *Met.* 1. 318 ff. Deucalion was the son of Prometheus. When Zeus flooded the earth in order to punish the sins of the Bronze Age, he and his wife Pyrrha built an ark and floated safely on it until the waters subsided. When the ark grounded, they were advised by Themis, or Hermes, to throw their mother's bones over their shoulders. They correctly took this to refer to the stones of the earth. From the stones thrown by Deucalion sprang up men, and from those thrown by Pyrrha women. The story figures among the illustrations quoted by St. Cyril in *Cat.* 12. 27.

⁷⁴ For objections of this sort, see Origen, *C. Cels.* 6. 73 (GCS 3. 142 = Chadwick 386 f.): 'But if He wanted to send down His spirit, why did He need to breathe it into a woman's womb? . . . He could have clothed it with a body without exposing His own spirit to such pollution.' St. Gregory of Nyssa mentions similar criticisms of the virgin birth, arguing in reply that there is nothing inherently impure in the reproductive organs (*Or. Cat.* 28: PG 45. 73). St. Augustine makes the same point against Manichaean objectors: cf. *C. Faust. Manich.* 29. 1 and 4 (CSEL 25. 743 f. and 746 f.). In *Cat.* 12. 25 f. St. Cyril seems to have in mind people who find the physical implications of our Lord's human birth distasteful.

⁷⁵ Both Origen (*C. Cels.* 6. 73: GCS 3. 143 = Chadwick 387) and St. Augustine (*De fide et symb.* 10: CSEL 41. 13 f.) use the illustration of the sun's rays to refute the objectors.

⁷⁶ Rufinus probably came across this theory, that the union between the divine and human natures in Christ was rendered possible by the spiritual constitution of His human soul, when translating Origen's *De principiis* in 398. Cf. *De princ.* 2. 6. 3. (GCS 22. 142: the passage survives in Rufinus's version): 'Hac ergo substantia animae inter Deum carnemque mediante (non enim possibile erat Dei naturam corpori sine mediatore misceri) nascitur, ut diximus, Deus-homo, illa substantia media existente, cui utique contra naturam non erat corpus assumere. Sed neque rursum anima illa, utpote substantia rationabilis, contra naturam habuit capere Deum.' See also *ibid.* 4. 4. 4 (GCS 22. 353). For the view, ultimately Neoplatonic in origin, that the soul stands midway between God and matter, we may compare

St. Augustine, *Tract. in Ioann. evang.* 20. 11 (PL 35. 1562): 'Tu si in animo es, in medio es. Si infra attendis, corpus est; si supra attendis, Deus est.' He made this the basis of his doctrine of the soul as the image of God. We may note that Cassian (*De Incarn.* 7. 27: CSEL 17. 385) singles out this sentence of Rufinus's for special commendation.

[77] The Old Roman Creed has 'Qui sub Pontio Pilato crucifixus est et sepultus,' and omits 'descendit ad inferna.' See n. 98 below.

[78] Rufinus here conflates Eph. 1. 18 and 3. 18. In the mystical interpretation of the cross which follows, he is clearly borrowing from St. Gregory of Nyssa, *Or. Cat.* 32 (PG 45. 81), who writes: 'It is from sight that the mighty Paul starts when he initiates the people of Ephesus in the mysteries, and by his instructions imbues them with the power of knowing what is that *depth and height and breadth and length.* In fact, he designates each projection of the cross by its proper appellation. The upper part he calls height, the lower depth, and the side extensions breadth and length; and in another passage he makes his thought still clearer to the Philippians, saying to them that *in the name of Jesus every knee should bow, of those that are in heaven, on earth, and under the earth.* In that passage he includes in one appellation the centre and projecting arms, calling *things on earth* all that is in the middle between things in heaven and things under the earth. Such is the lesson we learn in regard to the mystery of the cross.' Cf. a similar passage in *C. Eunom.* 5 (Jaeger 2. 115).

[79] For the suggestion that Christ's cross was a trophy, see St. Cyril, *Cat.* 13. 40: 'It was the trophy of salvation, the cross of Jesus, that brought you all together.' Cf. also Origen, *Comm. in Ioann.* 20. 36 (GCS 10. 376).

[80] Phil. 2. 10. As we observed above (n. 78), Rufinus was indebted to St. Gregory of Nyssa for his application of this text.

[81] For the belief, which goes back as least as far as St. Paul, who seems to have shared it (Eph. 2. 2, 6. 12), that the middle air was the habitat of demons, cf. A. Lemonnyer, 'L'air comme séjour d'anges d'après Philon,' *Rev. des sc. phil. et théol.* 1 (1907) 305 ff., and L. Gry, 'Séjours et habitats divins d'après les apocryphes de l'ancien testament,' *ibid.* 4 (1910) 694 ff. Cf. also M. Dibelius, *Die Geisterwelt im Glauben des Paulus* (Göttingen 1909) 156 f.; W. Foerster, 'δαίμων,' TWNT 2 (1935) 1-21. It is noteworthy that St. Athanasius counts it among the reasons for the suitability of the cross that Christ was thereby enabled to cleanse the air of the machinations of the devil, and so to open a road for men to ascend to heaven (*De Incarn.* 25: PG 25. 140).

[82] The reference is to Isa. 65. 2 ('I have spread forth my hands all the day to an unbelieving people, etc.'). The Fathers were fond of reading

this text as a prophecy of the crucifixion: cf. *Epistle of St. Barnabas* 12. 4 (Funk-Bihlmeyer 25 = ACW 6. 55); St. Justin, *Apol.* 1. 35 (Rauschen 1. 84); *Dial.* 97 (Archambault 2. 108): St. Irenaeus, *Epideixis* 79 (ed. J. A. Robinson 136 = ACW 16. 97); Tertullian, *Adv. Iud.* 13 (CSEL 70. 317); St. Cyprian, *Test.* 2. 20 (CSEL 3. 87); St. Athanasius, *De Incarn.* 38 (PG 25. 161); etc. St. Cyril quotes it in *Cat.* 13. 27.

[83] Deut. 32. 8. The Vulgate reads: 'Quando dividebat Altissimus gentes, . . . constituit terminos populorum *iuxta numerum filiorum Israel*,' which accurately reproduces the Hebrew original. Rufinus's Old Latin version depends on the Septuagint: ἔστησεν ὅρια ἐθνῶν κατὰ ἀριθμὸν ἀγγέλων Θεοῦ. Here the translator has introduced the notion of angelic rulers of the several nations of the world which is found in Dan. 10. 13, 20, 21, 12. 1; Ecclus. 17. 14. St. Jerome (*In Ezech.* 9. 28. 1 ff.: PL 25. 267) cites the Old Latin 'iuxta numerum angelorum Dei,' adding, 'sive, ut melius habetur in Hebraico, *iuxta numerum filiorum Israel.*' Origen, making this text his basis, argued that the division of the nations corresponded to the number of the angels: see *De princ.* 1. 5. 2; *Hom. in Num.* 11. 5 (GCS 22. 70; 30. 86). For an important discussion of the place of the doctrine in his cosmology, cf. J. Daniélou, *Origène* (Paris 1948) 222–35; also S. T. Bettencourt, *Doctrina ascetica Origenis, seu quid docuerit de ratione animae humanae cum daemonibus*, in *Studia Anselmiana* 16 (Rome 1945) 125–30. In later writers, e.g. Eusebius, *Dem. evang.* 4. 7 (GCS 23. 160 f.); St. Hilary, *Tract. in Ps.* 2. 31 (PL 9. 280), we find the developed theory that, while all the nations had been committed to the care of angels, Israel had been kept in the special charge of the Lord Himself.

[84] For the title, cf. John 12. 31, 14. 30, 16.11.

[85] Isa. 50. 1. The Vulgate reads: 'In iniquitatibus vestris venditi estis.' Rufinus gives the Old Latin, but inexactly, substituting the first person plural for the second.

[86] Col. 2. 14: an incomplete quotation.

[87] Ezech. 30. 9. Cf. the Vulgate: 'In die illa egredientur nuncii a facie mea in trieribus ad conterendam Aethiopiae confidentiam; et erit pavor in eis in die Aegypti, quia absque dubio veniet.' Rufinus's version exactly translates the Septuagint, interpreting ἄγγελοι (= 'messengers') as 'angels.'

[88] Luke 10.19. The text agrees with the Vulgate, except in giving 'super' for 'supra.'

[89] Phil. 2. 5–8. The Old Latin differs from the Vulgate in the omission of 'et' before 'in Christo Iesu' and in having 'habitu repertus' for 'habitu inventus.' Rufinus omits 'humiliavit semetipsum.'

[90] The theory that the essence of the Redemption consisted in Christ's

offering Himself as a ransom to the Devil in order to release mankind from the bondage of sin went back to Origen: cf. *Comm. in Matt.* 16. 8 (GCS 40. 2. 498 f.); *Hom. in Exod.* 6. 9 (GCS 29. 200); *In Rom.* 4. 11 (PG 14. 1000) etc.; see Bettencourt, *op. cit.* 20. The Devil over-reached himself in the transaction: he found that he could not hold the sinless soul of Christ. It was an easy step from this to the idea, expressed in this passage, of a deception deliberately practised on the Devil: this latter idea, although present in *Comm. in Matt.* 13. 9 (GCS 40. 1. 205), was hardly prominent in Origen's thought. St. Gregory of Nyssa, using the identical imagery of the fishhook, taught along these lines (*Or. Cat.* 24: PG 45. 65), and indeed it is likely that Rufinus borrowed from him. Crude though the conception was, it had a considerable vogue: cf. St. Leo, *Serm.* 22. 4 (PL 54. 197); St. Gregory the Great, *Mor.* 33. 14 (PL 76. 680), etc. St. Augustine altered the image to that of a mousetrap (*muscipula*): cf. *Serm.* 130. 2; 134. 6; 263. 1 (PL 38. 726; 745; 1210). The third of these passages ('he swallowed the bait as in a mousetrap') expresses the idea particularly neatly and forcibly.

[91] Rufinus alludes to Exod. 12. 7, where the Lord instructed Moses that the children of Israel should smear their doorposts with the blood of the Passover lamb, the type of Christ, saying (v. 13): *And the blood shall be unto you for a sign in the houses where you shall be: and I shall see the blood, and shall pass over you.*

[92] Ezech. 32. 3 f. The Vulgate reads: 'Et extraham te in sagena mea. Et proiciam te in terram, super faciem agri abiciam te, et habitare faciam super te omnia volatilia coeli, et satiabo de te bestias universae terrae.' St. Jerome (*In Ezech.* 32. 1 ff.: PL 25. 305) gives both texts, commenting: 'Editionem utramque miscemus, in his dumtaxat in quibus discrepant.'

[93] Ps. 73. 14. The Vulgate and Old Latin differ only in minute parti-culars.

[94] Job 40. 20. The Old Latin follows the Septuagint. The Vulgate reads: 'An extrahere poteris Leviathan hamo, et fune ligabis linguam eius?' St. Jerome quotes the Old Latin in *In Ezech.* 29. vv. 3 ff. and 32. vv. 1 ff. (PL 25. 279 and 307).

[95] Some MSS give a fuller text, viz. 'ad gentem in qua proprios habeat captivitatis vinculo alligatos, devictaque ea carcerem intret in quo devincti detinebantur, et ingressus etc.' The received text, as the editors of Migne point out, makes satisfactory sense without the addi-tional words, and there is nothing to suggest a gap.

[96] An echo of Ps. 106. 10.

[97] This formula goes back to St. Paul (cf. 1 Tim. 6. 13). It is almost a routine cliché in St. Ignatius (*Magn.* 11; *Trall.* 9. 1; *Smyrn.* 1. 2:

Funk-Bihlmeyer 91; 95; 106); St. Justin (*Apol.* 1. 13, 61, 2. 6 (Rauschen 24, 63, 96); *Dial.* 30; 76; 85 (Archambault 1. 132, 2. 10, 2. 56); St. Irenaeus (*Adv. haer.* 2. 49. 3, 3. 4. 1, 3. 12. 11, 5. 12. 4: Harvey 1. 375, 2. 16, 2. 62, 2. 354), and Tertullian (*De virg. vel.* 1.: Oehler 1. 884). What inspired the insertion of Pilate's name into the Church's creed was probably, as Rufinus suggests, the desire to emphasize that the redemptive story is rooted in history. JNDK 149 f.

[98] The Descent to Hell makes its first credal appearance in the Fourth Formula of Sirmium, the so-called Dated Creed of 359, and in the contemporary Homoean formulae published at Nicé and Constantinople which are dependent on it. The clause featured very early in Syrian quasi-credal material, and, although it never established itself in the official creeds of the East, it was probably under Eastern influence that it was admitted to Western formulae. It is included in some Spanish creeds of the sixth century, and was popular in Gallic creeds from the time of St. Caesarius of Arles onwards. In their original connotation the words probably did little more than emphasize the reality of Christ's death: according to Judaeo-Christian notions, the soul passed on death to the underworld, or Sheol. Such is the teaching implied, for example, in Tertullian's *De anima* 50 ff., esp. 55 (Waszink 67 ff., 73 f.). When later theologians speculated on Christ's activity in Hades, two streams of interpretation emerged. According to one, He spent His time preaching to those who had not had an opportunity of hearing His message; according to the other, which eventually prevailed in the West, He performed an act of triumphant liberation on behalf of the Old Testament saints. For the development of the theology of this clause, see H. Quilliet, 'Descente de Jésus aux enfers,' DTC 4. 1 (1939) 565–619. The motives for its introduction into the creed are obscure, although one conclusion that seems certain is that the old suggestion that its intention was anti-Apollinarian has no solid basis. It is perhaps significant that fourth-century theologians tended to see in the Descent the occasion of the vanquishing of death and the release by Christ of the saints held in its power. Cf. St. Cyril, *Cat.* 4. 11, 12. 15, 14. 17–19; also the Fourth Formula of Sirmium. On the whole question, see JNDK 378 ff. Rufinus, as his comment that the clause was equivalent to 'buried' shows, was clearly in the dark as to its real bearing and intention.

[99] 1 Cor. 1. 23 f. and 1 Cor. 1. 18.

[100] This whole paragraph, dealing with the unbelief of the Jews and the transference of God's favour from them to the Gentiles, is a loose paraphrase of St. Cyril, *Cat.* 13. 7.

[101] Isa. 52. 15. The Vulgate is different: 'Quibus non est narratum de
A.C.W.R.—9

eo, viderunt; et qui non audierunt, contemplati sunt.' The Old Latin of
Rufinus exactly reproduces the Septuagint, which St. Paul quotes in
Rom. 15. 21. St. Paul also saw in the text a prediction of the acceptance
of Christ by the Gentiles. St. Cyril applies it in the same connexion
(*Cat.* 13. 7).

[102] Isa. 25. 6 f. The Vulgate differs greatly: 'Et faciet Dominus
exercituum omnibus populis in monte hoc convivium pinguium, convivium vindemiae, pinguium medullatorum, vindemiae defaecatae. Et
praecipitabit in monte isto faciem vinculi colligati super omnes
populos, et telam quam orditus est super omnes nationes.' The Old
Latin exactly translates the Septuagint, except that it interpolates 'of the
Almighty.' St. Cyril (*Cat.* 21. 7) applies the prophecy to the Eucharist.

[103] Lam. 4. 20. The Old Latin, which Rufinus represents, existed in
several forms of text. The Vulgate reads: 'Spiritus oris nostri,' and
continues in the second person, 'cui diximus, In umbra tua etc.' The
text is cited by St. Cyril in the same connexion (*Cat.* 13. 7).

[104] The whole of the section 20-30 depends on St. Cyril, *Cat.*
13. 8 ff. Cf. the remark of St. Cyril's editor, P. Touttée in PG 33. 780
n. 4: 'Ita haec similia sunt iis quae apud Rufinum leguntur . . . ut
mihi nihil dubium sit, quin Rufinus ex istis Cyrilli fontibus suos
hortulos irrigarit. Eaedem sunt sententiae, eaedem Scripturarum in
eumdemque sensum allegationes, eodem ordine recitatae, eaedem
obiectiones, et ad obiecta responsiones. Mihi plane videtur totus ille
Rufini locus nihil aliud esse nisi libera et plane Rufiniana Cyrilli
interpretatio.'

[105] Ps. 40. 10. Cf. Vulgate: 'Qui edebat panes meos, magnificavit
super me supplantationem.' St. Cyril (*Cat.* 13. 9) does not cite this
text.

[106] *Ibid.* 37. 12. Cited by St. Cyril (*Cat.* 13. 9).

[107] *Ibid.* 54. 22. The text agrees with the Vulgate, except in reading
'will be darts' instead of 'are.' It is cited by St. Cyril (*Cat.* 13. 9).

[108] Matt. 26. 49. Rufinus seems to quote from memory: both the
Vulgate and the Old Latin read: 'Et confestim accedens ad Iesum
dixit, etc.' Cited by St. Cyril (*Cat.* 13. 9).

[109] Luke 22. 48. The text agrees with the Vulgate. St. Cyril cites the
verse (*Cat.* 13. 9).

[110] Zach. 11. 12 f. The Vulgate differs slightly, reading: 'et si non,
quiescite' for the Old Latin, 'aut abnuite,' and in v. 13: 'ad statuarium'
('to the statuary') for the Old Latin, 'ad conflatorium.' The latter
represents the Septuagint εἰς τὸ χωνευτήριον. The Syriac (Peshitta) has
'into the treasury,' which is almost certainly correct. The prophet,
having asked for his wages, receives from the people the paltry and

insulting sum of thirty shekels, the amount fixed in Exod. 21. 32 as the compensation for an injured slave. As if to show that it is Yahweh Himself, whom the prophet represents, to whom they are paying so wretched a sum, he is commanded to throw it into the Temple treasury. St. Cyril cites the passage in *Cat.* 13. 10, and in the following chapter dwells at length on the relation between the foundry mentioned here and the potter's field which the chief priests purchased with the thirty pieces of silver (Matt. 27. 7 ff.).

[111] Cf. Matt. 27. 3 ff.

[112] Isa. 3. 9 f. The Vulgate has no mention of binding: 'Vae animae eorum, quoniam reddita sunt eis mala. Dicite iusto quoniam bene, quoniam fructum adinventionum suarum comedet.' The Old Latin, which is also quoted by St. Ambrose (*De ben. patr.* 3. 13: PL 14. 677) as a prediction of our Lord's passion, translates the Septuagint, which seems to incorporate a reminiscence of Wisd. 2. 12 (*Let us therefore lie in wait for the just, because he is not for our turn*—δύσχρηστος, as in the Septuagint version of our context). St. Cyril appeals to the same passage (*Cat.* 13. 12).

[113] *Ibid.* 3. 14. The Vulgate has: 'Cum senibus populi sui et principibus eius.' St. Cyril applies the passage to Our Lord's trial (*Cat.* 13. 12).

[114] Isa. 53. 1. The Vulgate omits 'Domine.' St. Cyril quotes the same passage after speaking of the buffeting, spitting, etc. which Our Lord endured (*Cat.* 13. 13).

[115] Isa. 50. 6. The Old Latin faithfully reproduces the Septuagint. The Vulgate is differently worded, reading 'corpus meum' for 'dorsum meum,' and 'ab increpantibus et conspuentibus in me' for 'a confusione sputorum.' St. Cyril quotes it in the same connexion (*Cat.* 13. 13). This is one of the passages of prophecy in which, according to the teaching of the Catholic Church, God (i.e. the second Person of the Holy Trinity) has placed His own words in the prophet's mouth. So when St. Jerome comments on it (*In Is. proph.* 50. 4 ff.: PL 24. 478 f.), he indignantly rejects the Jewish suggestion that the words must be referred to the person of Isaias himself, and goes on to demonstrate how aptly they apply to the Saviour, who is foretelling through the prophet His own humiliations.

[116] Osee 10. 6. The Vulgate reads: 'Siquidem et ipse in Assur delatus est, munus regi ultori.' Rufinus's Old Latin depends on the Septuagint: καὶ αὐτὸν (εἰς 'Ασσυρίους) δήσαντες ἀπήνεγκαν ξένια τῷ βασιλεῖ 'Ιαρείμ. In the original the reference is to the Calf of Bethel, which Osee prophesies will be carried away as a present, i.e. as tribute. The meaning of the mysterious words rendered 'regi ultori' (Vulg.) or 'regi Jarim' (O.L. & LXX: 'Jareb' is truer to the Hebrew) is obscure:

for a list of the many interpretations conjectured, see W. R. Harper, *Amos and Hosea* (*International Critical Commentary*), *ad loc.* The probability is that it stands here, as in Osee 5. 13, for some unknown proper name, or a nickname (G. A. Smith proposed 'King Pick-Quarrel'), or (distributing the letters differently and reading *malkī rābh*) for 'the Great King,' i.e. the contemporary Assyrian monarch. St. Cyril cites the text as a prophecy of our Lord's being haled before Pilate, and follows it with the same hypothetical objection on the score of Pilate's not being a king (*Cat.* 13. 14). The text was also taken as a prediction of Luke 23. 7 by St. Justin (*Dial.* 103: Archambault 2. 138) and Tertullian (*Adv. Marc.* 4. 42: CSEL 47. 563).

¹¹⁷ Luke 23. 6 f. A loose paraphrase from memory.

¹¹⁸ Rufinus took 'Jarim' ('Ιαρείμ in the Septuagint), which he read in the Old Latin, as equivalent to the Hebrew 'ye'arim' ('woods,' 'forests'). Herod Antipas, the son of Herod the Great, belonged to a family which was in origin Idumaean (i.e. from Edom), and therefore alien to, and hated by, the pure Jewish stock.

¹¹⁹ Isa. 5. 1. The Vulgate reads 'filio olei' in place of the Old Latin's 'in loco uberi.'

¹²⁰ Job 12. 24. The Vulgate has: 'Qui immutat cor principum populi terrae.' 'Reconciliat' of Rufinus's Old Latin reflects διαλλάσσων in the Septuagint. St. Cyril quotes the passage to make the same point about the reconciliation of Pilate and Herod (*Cat.* 13. 14).

¹²¹ Luke 23. 21. Cf. St. Cyril, *Cat.* 13. 15.

¹²² Jer. 12. 8 and 7. The wording of the Vulgate differs in small details. St. Cyril (*Cat.* 13. 15) cites the text.

¹²³ Isa. 57. 4. Old Latin and Septuagint. Cf. Vulgate: 'Super quem dilatastis os et eiecistis linguam?' Cited by St. Cyril (*Cat.* 13. 15).

¹²⁴ Matt. 26. 63.

¹²⁵ Ps. 37. 15 and 14. In v. 15 the Vulgate substitutes 'redargutiones' for the Old Latin 'increpationes.' In v. 14 Rufinus practically agrees with the Vulgate. St. Cyril cites both verses in the same order as predictions of Our Lord's silence (*Cat.* 13. 16).

¹²⁶ Isa. 53. 7 f. In v. 7 the Vulgate gives the future ('aperiet') where the Old Latin has the past ('aperuit'): the Septuagint gives the present (ἀνοίγει), and the past is probably the result of the influence of the preceding verb 'was led.' The Vulgate gives a rather different reading for v. 8: 'De angustia et de iudicio sublatus est.' The Old Latin follows the Septuagint. The text is not cited by St. Cyril, *Cat.* 13. 16, although he refers to it in 10. 3.

¹²⁷ Cant. 3. 11. The quotation is somewhat loose: the original, in both the Vulgate and the Old Latin versions, runs: *Go forth, ye daughters*

of Sion, and see King Solomon in the diadem (O.L. '*crown*') *wherewith his people crowned him in the day of his espousals*. St. Cyril also read the text as a forecast of the crown of thorns (*Cat.* 13. 17).

[128] Isa. 5. 2 and 7. In v. 2 the Vulgate gives the third person ('expectavit'), and reads 'wild grapes' ('labruscas') for the Old Latin 'spinas' (Septuagint: ἀκάνθας). In v. 7 it has, 'Behold, a cry.' St. Cyril does not cite the text in *Cat.* 13. 17 f., but alludes to it as prophesying the crown of thorns in *Cat.* 13. 29.

[129] Gen. 3. 17 f. The Vulgate has the singular: 'in opere tuo.' St. Cyril gives exactly the same theological explanation of the crown of thorns, adding that Christ's burial in the earth had a similar effect (*Cat.* 13. 18).

[130] Jer. 11. 19. Cf. the Vulgate: 'Mittamus lignum in panem eius, et eradamus eum de terra viventium.' If the Hebrew text is correct as it stands, the meaning would seem to be: 'Let us destroy the tree with its fruit,' the word 'bread' being taken as signifying 'fruit,' a usage to which there are said to be Arabic parallels. Some suggest making a slight emendation which would give the translation 'sap.' The Septuagint mistranslated 'destroy' by ἐκβαλῶμεν. The Fathers found a key to the mysterious sentence by taking 'bread' as meaning Our Lord's sacred Body, and so eliciting a prediction of the laying of the cross on His shoulders on the road to Calvary. Cf. St. Justin, *Dial.* 72 (Archambault 1. 348); Tertullian, *Adv. Iud.* 10; *C. Marc.* 3. 19, 4. 40 (CSEL 70. 306; 47. 408, 560); St. Cyprian, *Test.* 2. 15 (CSEL 3. 1. 80); St. Athanasius, *De Incarn.* 35 (PG 25. 156); St. Cyril, *Cat.* 13. 19.

[131] Deut. 28. 66. The Vulgate has: 'quasi pendens ante te.' Cited by St. Cyril, *Cat.* 13. 19. The Fathers generally applied this text mystically to Our Lord's crucifixion. So St. Irenaeus, *Adv. haer.* 4. 20. 2, 5. 18. 2 (Harvey 2. 174, 375); Tertullian, *Adv. Iud.* 13 (CSEL 70. 318); St. Cyprian, *Test.* 2. 20 (CSEL 3. 1. 87); St. Athanasius, *De Incarn.* 35 (PG 25. 156); St. Augustine, *C. Faust. Manich.* 16. 5 (CSEL 25. 442); Ambrosiaster, *In ep. 1 ad Cor.* 15. 3 (PL 17. 261).

[132] John 19. 34. St. Cyril cites the incident in *Cat.* 13. 21: Rufinus's mystical interpretation of it is simply a paraphrase of St. Cyril's.

[133] *Ibid.* 7. 38. The Vulgate reads 'fluent' for Rufinus's 'procedent.' Our Lord applied these words to those who were going to believe in Him.

[134] Cf. Matt. 27. 25: *And the whole people answering, said: His blood be upon us and upon our children.*

[135] Cf. St. Cyril, *Cat.* 13. 21: 'For since in the Gospels the power of saving baptism is twofold, one which is granted by means of water to the illuminated, and a second to holy martyrs, in persecutions, through

their own blood, there came out of that blessed side blood and water.' The view early established itself in the Church that the martyr's death conveyed all the regenerative effects of baptism: cf. Origen, *Hom. in Iud.* 7. 2 (GCS 30. 507): 'It is only the baptism of blood which can render us purer than the baptism of water has done.' See also Tertullian, *De bapt.* 16 (CSEL 20. 214); St. Cyprian, *Ep.* 73. 22 (CSEL 3. 2. 795 f.); St. Cyril, *Cat.* 3. 10; St. Augustine, *De civ. Dei* 13. 7 (CSEL 40. 1. 622 ff.). St. Augustine's words deserve quotation: 'For whatever unbaptized persons die confessing Christ, their confession has the same efficacy for the remission of sins as if they were washed in the sacred font of baptism. For He who said, *Unless a man be born again of water and the Holy Spirit, he cannot enter into the kingdom of God*, made an exception in their favour in that other and no less absolute sentence of His, *Everyone that shall confess me before men, I will also confess him before my Father who is in heaven*, and again in the words, *He that shall lose his life for my sake shall find it*. And this explains the verse, *Precious in the sight of the Lord is the death of His saints*. For what is more precious than a death by which a man's sins are all forgiven and his merits increased a hundredfold? For those who had been baptized when they could no longer escape death, and have departed this life with all their sins blotted out, surely do not enjoy equal merit with those who did not defer death, though it was in their power to do so, but preferred to end their life by confessing Christ.'

[136] Cf. St. Cyril, *Cat.* 13. 21: 'There is also another reason for mentioning His side. The woman was the first beginning of sin, and she was formed out of the side. So when Jesus came to bestow forgiveness on men and women alike, He was pierced in His side on behalf of women, so as to undo their sin.'

[137] Cf. Matt. 27. 45. St. Cyril deals with the darkness in *Cat.* 13. 24: Rufinus borrows his argument in all its detail from him.

[138] Amos 8. 9. The Vulgate omits 'tibi.' The text was frequently cited by the Fathers as foretelling the darkness during the Passion: cf. St. Irenaeus, *Adv. haer.* 4. 33. 12 (Harvey 4. 55. 2); Tertullian, *Adv. Iud.* 10 (CSEL 70. 308); St. Cyprian, *Test.* 2. 23 (CSEL 3. 1. 91); etc.

[139] Zach. 14. 6 f.: a prophecy of the commencement of the Messianic age. The Old Latin differs in small details from the Vulgate: the original is uncertain.

[140] Cf. John 18. 18; Mark 14. 67.

[141] Amos 8. 9. The Vulgate reads: 'Et tenebrescere faciam terram in die luminis.'

[142] Cf. Matt. 27. 35. St. Cyril deals with the incident along similar lines in *Cat.* 13. 26.

[143] Ps. 21. 19. The Vulgate and the Old Latin agree. The text is cited as a prediction by the Evangelist himself (Matt. 27. 35).

[144] Isa. 63. 1 f. The Vulgate differs: '. . . tinctis vestibus de Bosra? . . . 2. Quare ergo rubrum est indumentum tuum, et vestimenta tua sicut calcantium in torculari?' Again Rufinus is modelling his argument on St. Cyril (*Cat.* 13. 27).

[145] *Ibid.* 63. 3. The words 'filiae Sion' are not in the text either of the Vulgate or of the Old Latin. St. Cyril does not quote the verse: the reading of the Septuagint (πλήρης καταπεπατημένης) was not suitable.

[146] An echo of Rom. 5. 12 ff.

[147] Ps. 68. 22. The Vulgate text agrees. St. Cyril cites the verse in the same connexion (*Cat.* 13. 29).

[148] Deut. 32. 32. Cf. Vulgate: 'De vinea Sodomorum, vinea eorum, et de suburbanis Gomorrhae; uva eorum uva fellis, et botri amarissimi.' St. Cyril also appealed to this verse: *Cat.* 13. 29.

[149] *Ibid.* 32. 6. The Vulgate gives much the same text. St. Cyril cites the verse in connexion with the buffeting and spitting which took place earlier in the Passion: cf. *Cat.* 13. 13.

[150] Cant. 5. 1. Cf. Vulgate: 'Veni in hortum meum, soror mea, sponsa; messui myrrham meam.' Rufinus found the verse quoted by St. Cyril, *Cat.* 13. 32.

[151] Cf. Matt. 27. 50.

[152] Ps. 30. 6. The Vulgate and the Old Latin agree. Cf. St. Cyril, *Cat.* 13. 33.

[153] Lam. 3. 53: 'Mortificaverunt in lacum vitam meam.' Cf. Vulgate: 'Lapsa est in lacum vita mea.' Rufinus's Old Latin follows the Septuagint, which reads: ἐθανάτωσαν ἐν λάκκῳ ζωήν μου. The primary meaning of the Hebrew seems to be: 'They have cut off my life in the dungeon,' the reference being to the prophet's experiences described in Jer. 37. 14 ff. St. Cyril quotes the text in *Cat.* 13. 35.

[154] Isa. 57. 1 f. The Vulgate reads: 'A facie enim malitiae collectus est iustus. Veniat pax, requiescat in cubili suo. . . .' The Septuagint, on which the Old Latin is based, has: 'His burial place (ἡ ταφὴ αὐτοῦ) will be in peace.' The correct sense of the Hebrew seems to be: 'The righteous man is carried off (by violent death) as a result of wickedness, and enters into peace,' i.e. descends to the grave. The words are cited by St. Cyril in *Cat.* 14. 3, when he resumes his discussion of Our Lord's burial.

[155] *Ibid.* 53. 9. Cf. Vulgate: 'Et dabit impios pro sepultura.' The original means: 'They made his grave with the wicked.' In reading 'dabo' and 'malignos' Rufinus's Old Latin follows the Septuagint. St. Cyril cites the verse in *Cat.* 14. 3.

[156] Gen. 49. 9. The text agrees with the Septuagint, except in giving the third person ('dormivit') instead of the second (ἐκοιμήθης). The Vulgate reads: 'Recubans accubuisti ut leo et quasi leaena. Quis suscitabit eum?' The text was frequently applied to Our Lord's death, e.g. by St. Hilary, *Tract. in Ps.* 131. 8 (PL 9. 733), and St. Ambrose, *De ben. patr.* 4. 20 (PL 14. 679 f.). St. Cyril cites it in *Cat.* 14. 3.

[157] Ps. 21. 16. The Vulgate text agrees. Cf. St. Cyril, *Cat.* 14. 3.

[158] *Ibid.* 29. 10. The Vulgate text agrees, except in giving 'descendo' where Rufinus has 'descendero.' The verse is not quoted by St. Cyril.

[159] *Ibid.* 68. 3. Instead of 'Descendi in limum profundi,' the Vulgate has 'Infixus sum in limo profundi.' Not cited by St. Cyril.

[160] Luke 7. 20. In fact, the point of St. John Baptist's inquiry was to confirm that Our Lord was the One mightier than he, whose coming he had foretold (Matt. 3. 11; Mark 1. 7; Luke 3. 16). The Fathers often applied the question to the Baptist's meeting with Our Lord in the underworld: cf., e.g., St. Cyril, *Cat.* 14. 19; St. John Chrysostom, *In Matt. hom.* 36. 3 (PG 57. 416).

[161] 1 Peter 3. 18–20: a loose quotation, probably from memory. For the Descent to Hell and Rufinus's ideas about it, see n. 98 above, and also what he says in the following chapter.

[162] Ps. 15. 10. The text is identical with that of the Vulgate, except in reading 'quia' for 'quoniam.' St. Cyril cites the verse in *Cat.* 14. 4.

[163] *Ibid.* 29. 4. The Vulgate has slight differences in word order. St. Cyril cites the verse in *Cat.* 14. 4.

[164] *Ibid.* 15. 10. See n. 162 above.

[165] Rufinus closely follows St. Cyril, who writes (*Cat.* 14. 18 f.): 'He descended to hell alone, but ascended hither with a great company. For He went down to death, and many bodies of saints who had fallen asleep were raised through Him (Matt. 27. 52). Death was struck with dismay on beholding a new visitant descended to the underworld, not bound by the chains of that place. . . . Death fled, and his flight betrayed his cowardice. The holy prophets ran unto Him, with Moses the lawgiver, and Abraham, and Isaac, and Jacob. David also, and Samuel, and Isaias, and John the Baptist, who bore witness when he asked, *Art thou he that art to come, or look we for another?* So all the just ones whom Death had swallowed up, were ransomed. For it was appropriate that the King whom they had proclaimed should become the redeemer of His noble heralds.' The view that the patriarchs, prophets, and righteous men were redeemed by Christ in Hades appears in St. Irenaeus, *Adv. haer.* 1. 25. 2, 4. 42. 4 (Harvey 1. 218 f., 2. 241); Clement of Alexandria, *Strom.* 6. 6 (GCS 15. 453 ff.); Origen, *In Gen. hom.* 15. 5 (GCS 29. 133 f.); Eusebius, *Dem. ev.* 4. 12 (GCS

23. 169 f.); St. Epiphanius, *Haer.* 69. 64 (GCS 37. 213); St. John Chrysostom, *In Matt. hom.* 36. 3 (PG 57. 416 f.).

[166] John 12. 32. The Vulgate differs in word order, and opens with, 'Et ego, si exaltatus fuero,' instead of, 'Cum exaltatus fuero.'

[167] Matt. 27. 52 f. The quotation is abbreviated, and there are slight verbal differences from the Vulgate. Referred to by St. Cyril, *Cat.* 14. 18.

[168] Gal. 4. 26. The Vulgate has simply, 'mater nostra,' which represents the authentic Greek text, which probably lacked πάντων.

[169] Heb. 2. 10. The Vulgate text agrees exactly.

[170] Eph. 2. 6. Cf. the Vulgate: 'Et conresuscitavit nos, et consedere fecit.'

[171] Jer. 18. 4. The Vulgate has: 'Et dissipatum est vas, quod ipse faciebat e luto manibus suis; conversusque fecit illud vas alterum, sicut placuerat in oculis eius ut faceret.' Rufinus quotes loosely from a version based on the Septuagint. The passage is not cited by St. Cyril.

[172] *psalmographus* (ψαλμογράφος), 'psalmist'—one who writes or composes psalms. The word seems to antedate (cf. Ps.-Tertullian, *Carmen adv. Marcionitas* 3. 130—before 325 A.D.) the more usual *psalmista* (ψαλμιστής), 'psalmist,'—one who writes or sings psalms (Hilary of Poitiers, Ambrose, Jerome, Augustine, etc.); cf. C. Mohrmann, *Die altchristliche Sondersprache in den Sermones des hl. Augustin*, LCP 3 (1932) 140.

[173] Osee 3. 6. So the Vulgate, except that it gives 'quia' for 'quoniam' in Rufinus's Old Latin.

[174] Ps. 11. 6. The Vulgate agrees. The passage is cited by St. Cyril (*Cat.* 14. 4), In his survey of prophecies of the Resurrection which follows, Rufinus draws largely on St. Cyril's much fuller treatment in *Cat.* 14.

[175] *Ibid.* 29. 4. So the Vulgate, except that it gives 'ab inferno' where Rufinus reads 'de inferno.' Cf. St. Cyril, *Cat.* 14. 4.

[176] *Ibid.* 70. 20. So the Vulgate, except that it gives 'de abyssis' where Rufinus reads 'de abysso.'

[177] *Ibid.* 87. 5. The Septuagint, Vulgate, and Old Latin all agree with the original in giving the first person, 'I am become. . . .' The verse was a favourite with St. Cyril: cf. *Cat.* 13. 34, 14. 1, 14. 8.

[178] Osee 6. 3. Cf. the Vulgate: 'Vivificabit nos post duos dies: in die tertia suscitabit nos, et vivemus in conspectu eius.' The text was widely accepted by the Fathers as a prediction of the Resurrection: cf. Tertullian, *Adv. Marc.* 4. 43 (CSEL 47. 565 f.); St. Cyprian, *Test.* 2. 25 (CSEL 3. 1. 92); St. Augustine, *De civ. Dei* 18. 28 (CSEL 40. 2. 306); etc. St. Cyril quotes it in *Cat.* 14. 14.

[179] Isa 63. 11. The Vulgate offers a different text: 'Ubi est qui eduxit eos de mari cum pastoribus gregis sui?' This accurately represents the received Hebrew text, the original reference probably being to the rescue of Israel from the Red Sea by its two shepherds, Moses and Aaron. The Versions, however, and some Hebrew MSS suggest a reading closer to that familiar to Rufinus, viz. 'Where is He that brought up from the sea the shepherd of His flock?' If this is the authentic primitive text, as seems to be the case, the reference must be to the rescue of Moses as a child from the Nile described in Exod. 2. In the Septuagint, on which Rufinus's Old Latin is based, this appears with ἐκ τῆς θαλάσσης (which is the reading of Codex Vaticanus gr. 1209) changed to ἐκ τῆς γῆς. In this form it was quoted by St. Athanasius (*Ad Serap.* 1. 12: PG 26. 560 f.) and others, as well as by St. Cyril (*Cat.* 14. 20), being naturally interpreted as foreshadowing the Resurrection. Under the influence of the Septuagint, St. Paul echoes this passage in Heb. 13. 20 (*. . . the God of peace, who brought again from the dead the great Pastor of the sheep, our Lord Jesus Christ*), and it is to him that the interpolation of the adjective 'great' is due.

[180] *Ibid.* 27. 11. The Vulgate differs: 'mulieres venientes, et docentes eam.' Rufinus's version translates the Septuagint. St. Cyril cites the verse in the same connexion (*Cat.* 14. 14).

[181] John 20. 13. Rufinus omits 'meum.' St. Cyril mentions the incident in *Cat.* 14. 12.

[182] Cant. 3. 1. So the Vulgate, with slight variations. Cf. St. Cyril, *Cat.* 14. 12.

[183] *Ibid.* 3. 4. Cf. Vulgate: 'Tenui eum, nec dimittam.' The words 'whom my soul loveth' belong to the preceding sentence in the original. St. Cyril applies the text similarly to the Gospel incident (*Cat.* 14. 12 f.).

[184] Rufinus is concerned in this passage to point out that a firm grasp of what was later to be called the doctrine of the Two Natures is essential to an understanding of the Ascension, Session, and Second Coming. If we overlook the fact that the Son eternally abides in the Father in His divine nature, we shall slip into the error of regarding Him as a mere man raised to the divine level by adoption. Cf. n. 191 below.

[185] Ps. 67. 19. The Vulgate reads: 'Ascendisti in altum, cepisti captivitatem, accepisti dona in hominibus.' The verse is quoted in the form reproduced by Rufinus in Eph 4. 8. St. Cyril cites it in the same form in *Cat.* 14. 24, where he treats of the Ascension. St. Paul's version, reading 'gave gifts' instead of the Hebrew original's 'didst receive gifts,' seems to have been based on a Jewish paraphrase of the Psalm: see H. Strack-P. Billerbeck, *Kommentar zum Neuen Testament aus Talmud und Midrasch* 3 (Munich 1926) 596.

[186] Acts 2. 33. Rufinus abbreviates the text. Cf. the Vulgate: 'Dextera igitur Dei exaltatus, et promissione Spiritus Sancti accepta a Patre, effudit hunc, quem vos videtis et auditis.'

[187] Ps. 23. 7. The Vulgate is practically identical. The correct translation of the Hebrew is: 'Lift up your heads, O ye gates.' The Vulgate reading, like Rufinus's, was suggested by the Septuagint, ἄρατε πύλας, οἱ ἄρχοντες, ὑμῶν, and arose from the order of the Hebrew words. The verse is cited by St. Cyril, *Cat.* 14. 24.

[188] *Ibid.* 46. 6. The Vulgate has 'in jubilo' for Rufinus's 'in jubilatione.' Cited by St. Cyril, *Cat.* 14. 24.

[189] Amos 9. 6. So the Vulgate. Cf. St. Cyril, *Cat.* 14. 24.

[190] Ps. 17. 11. The text, which agrees with the Vulgate, has been shortened by the omission of 'et volavit' after 'Cherubim.'

[191] Rufinus here takes a somewhat different, more subtle line than his master. St. Cyril places great emphasis on Christ's eternal session, criticizing the suggestion of certain heretics that 'it was after His cross, resurrection, and ascension into heaven that the Son began to sit on the Father's right hand.' He proceeds: 'It was not by any promotion that the Son acquired His throne; but throughout His being (and His being is by an eternal generation) He also sitteth together with the Father.' So *Cat.* 14. 27–30: cf. also *Cat.* 4. 7, 11. 17. Rufinus, on the other hand, draws a distinction, as we observed in the preceding chapter, between (a) the Word's eternal existence in the Father, and (b) the session of the Word made flesh at the Father's right hand.

[192] Ps. 92. 2. The Vulgate is practically identical. St. Cyril cites the verse (*Cat.* 14. 27) as a proof of the eternal session.

[193] Phil. 2. 10 f. The Vulgate omits 'to Him,' and has 'Christ' after 'Jesus' as well as inserting the verb 'est.'

[194] Ps. 109. 1. The Vulgate is identical. Cf. St. Cyril, *Cat.* 14. 28.

[195] Matt. 22. 45. The Vulgate, like what is almost certainly (in spite of a goodly number of MSS, versions, and authors) the Greek original, lacks 'in spirit.' Rufinus may have borrowed his version from St. Cyril, who quotes it (*Cat.* 14. 28) in the form πῶς οὖν Δαβὶδ ἐν πνεύματι κύριον αὐτὸν καλεῖ; The reading may have been influenced by Mark 12. 36. Rufinus takes the words 'in spiritu' as meaning 'in respect of His spirit,' i.e. that Christ is Lord in His divine nature.

[196] *Ibid.* 26. 64. The Vulgate gives 'a dextris' for Rufinus's 'ad dexteram.' Cf. St. Cyril, *Cat.* 14. 29.

[197] I Peter 3. 22. The Vulgate, in harmony with the Greek (πορευθεὶς εἰς οὐρανόν), reads 'profectus in coelum.' Cf. St. Cyril, *Cat.* 14. 29.

[198] Eph. 1. 19 f. The Vulgate has '. . . suscitans illum (Rufinus:

"eum") a mortuis, et constituens ad dexteram suam (Rufinus: "sedere faciens in dextera sua").' Cf. St. Cyril, *Cat.* 14. 29.

[199] Ps. 111. 5. The Vulgate lack 'quia,' and gives the future 'disponet.'

[200] For this curious interpretation of 'living and dead' (cf. 1 Tim. 4. 1), see St. Isidore of Pelusium (*ca.* 360–*ca.* 435), *Ep.* 1. 222 (PG 78. 321): 'By the judgment of living and dead is meant that both soul and body come to judgment together, and not separately. Just as they formed a unity here, so they will undergo judgment in unison there.' St. Augustine, in *Enchiridion* 55 (PL 40. 258), offers two alternative explanations: *The living and the dead* comprise either those who are alive at the Second Coming along with those who have already died, or the just and the unjust. For the same explanations, see his *De fide et symb.* 15 (CSEL 41. 17). St. Cyril (*Cat.* 15. 26) adopts the interpretation which Rufinus rejects.

[201] Matt. 10. 28. The quotation is loose, and seems to echo Luke 12. 4. In Matt. 10. 28 the Vulgate reads: 'animam autem non possunt occidere,' and in Luke 12. 4, 'et post haec non habent amplius quid faciant.'

[202] Mal. 3. 1–3. Cf. Vulgate: 'Ecce venit, dicit Dominus exercituum. Et quis poterit cogitare diem adventus eius, et quis stabit ad videndum eum? Ipse enim quasi ignis conflans, et quasi herba fullonum; et sedebit conflans et emundans argentum.' Rufinus's Old Latin (a text closely akin to it appears in St. Ambrose, *In ps. enarr.* 36. 26: PL 14. 980) reflects the Septuagint: the latter, however, like St. Ambrose, gives the present 'He comes' (ἔρχεται), which some MSS read here. The verses are cited by St. Cyril, *Cat.* 15. 2.

[203] Dan. 7. 13 f. The Vulgate differs in detail, reading 'antiquum dierum' for the older form 'vetustum dierum,' 'obtulerunt eum' for 'oblatus est,' and 'dedit ei potestatem, etc.' for 'et ipse datus est, etc.' The Old Latin follows the Septuagint. Cf. St. Cyril, *Cat.* 15. 27.

[204] The Aquileian creed in fact did not contain this clause. Rufinus quotes it by an oversight: he must have been thinking of the creed of Jerusalem commented on by St. Cyril: cf. *Cat.* 15. 27 ff. The heretical teaching against which the words are directed is that of Marcellus of Ancyra (died *ca.* 374), who held that Christ's kingdom must one day be brought to an end, quoting as his authority the Pauline text (1 Cor. 15. 25): *For He must reign, until He hath put all His enemies under His feet.* Marcellus was in effect a Sabellian, teaching that the divine Monad, which in the process of revelation had unfolded itself successively so as to form a Triad, would eventually return, by an ordered reversal of the process, to its original unity, so that God would be all in

all. He seems to have denied the existence of permanent hypostatic distinctions within the being of the Godhead. He had been an ardent champion of the Homoousion at the council of Nicaea and in the decades following, but his support proved embarrassing to the orthodox party: their opponents tended to confuse the Nicene theology with his type of Modalism. Anti-Marcellan clauses, cast in these or similar terms (the words in question are borrowed from Luke 1. 33), were incorporated in most of the conciliar creeds constructed in the middle years of the fourth century. The surviving fragments of his writings have been assembled by E. Klostermann in GCS 14. 185–215.

²⁰⁵ John 5. 43. The Vulgate lacks 'quia,' and reads 'non accepistis' for 'non recepistis,' and 'si alius venerit' for 'alius veniet.' Cited by St. Cyril, *Cat.* 12. 2.

²⁰⁶ Matt. 24. 15. The Vulgate has 'quae dicta est a Daniele propheta.' Cited by St. Cyril, *Cat.* 15. 9.

²⁰⁷ 2 Thess. 2. 3 f. The Vulgate differs in minor details.

²⁰⁸ *Ibid.* 2. 8 f. The Vulgate has 'destruet illustratione adventus sui' for Rufinus's 'evacuabit eum illuminatione adventus sui,' and 'operationem Satanae' for his 'opera Satanae.' St. Cyril cites the passage in the same connexion in *Cat.* 15. 9: indeed, this whole section is closely modelled on St. Cyril. In the latter's view, the heresies of his time represented the prophesied general apostasy, and he looked for the coming of a personal Antichrist 'when the times of the Roman empire shall have been fulfilled, and the end of the world draws nigh.' Cf. *Cat.* 15. 10 ff.

²⁰⁹ *Ibid.* 2. 10 f. The Vulgate agrees exactly.

²¹⁰ Matt. 24. 23 f. The quotation is loose: cf. the Vulgate: 'Tunc si quis vobis dixerit: Ecce hic est Christus, aut illic, nolite credere. Surgent enim pseudochristi et pseudoprophetae, et dabunt signa magna, etc.' Cited by St. Cyril, *Cat.* 15. 9 and 10.

²¹¹ *Ibid.* 24. 27. A loose quotation: cf. the Vulgate: 'Sicut enim fulgur exit ab oriente et paret usque in occidentem, ita erit et adventus Filii hominis.' Cited by St. Cyril, *Cat.* 15. 10.

²¹² *Ibid.* 25. 32. A loose quotation: the Vulgate reads: 'Et separabit eos ab invicem, sicut pastor segregat oves ab haedis.' Cf. St. Cyril, *Cat.* 15. 25.

²¹³ 2 Cor. 5. 10. The Vulgate differs, reading 'omnes enim nos manifestari' for Rufinus's 'quia omnes nos stare,' 'ut referat' for his 'ut recipiat,' and 'sive bonum sive malum' for his 'sive bona sive mala.'

²¹⁴ Rom. 2. 15 f. The Vulgate agrees, except that it has 'in die cum' where Rufinus reads 'in die quo.' St. Cyril cites the text in *Cat.* 15. 25.

[215] In the eyes of Rufinus, living in an age of mature theological development, the creed seemed primarily an expression of Trinitarian orthodoxy. Hence the narrative of Christ's experiences which filled out the second article seemed to him to interrupt the exposition of the theology of the three Persons of the eternal Godhead. As a matter of fact, although they were Trinitarian in form and implication, it had not been the original object of Western baptismal creeds to set forth the theology of the Trinity as such. Their Trinitarian pattern corresponded to, and was imposed by, the triple questions and answers which formed the core of the baptismal rite, and ultimately derived from the Saviour's command to baptize in Matt. 28. 19. Rufinus's instinct was correct in suspecting that the Christological narrative was an intrusion. There is plenty of evidence that in the second century, as well as earlier, Christological summaries circulated freely as independent, single-clause confessions of faith. The decisive moment in the evolution of the Old Roman Creed was when one of these was inserted bodily into a simple, originally independent, Trinitarian baptismal formula. On the whole question see JNDK chs. 3 and 4.

[216] Rufinus practically translates St. Cyril at this point. Cf. Cat. 16. 3: 'There is but one Holy Spirit, the Paraclete. Just as God the Father is one, and there is no second Father; and just as there is one only-begotten Son and Word of God, and He has no brother; so the Holy Spirit is one only, and there is no second Spirit of equal honour with Him.' It is somewhat surprising, in view of the controversies about the status of the Holy Spirit in the Godhead which had only been settled a generation before at the council of Constantinople (381), that Rufinus did not think it appropriate to include a reasoned argument for the orthodox doctrine which he was summarizing.

[217] The reading of some MSS and editors is 'tanquam de utroque procedens.' Although favoured by Migne, this probably represents an emendation made by a later scribe or editor accustomed to the Western teaching of the Double Procession of the Holy Spirit from the Father and the Son. St. Augustine was the first to give a clear and reasoned statement of the Double Procession: see, for example, De trin 4. 29 (PL 42. 908). Of Rufinus's contemporaries St. Ambrose, while teaching clearly that the Son is the principle of the Spirit's being (cf. De Spir. sanct. 1. 152, 2. 118: PL 16. 739, 768), was very guarded in his language about the Procession. The use of 'tanquam' in our passage certainly suggests that Rufinus was conscious of speaking metaphorically. The view that 'de Dei ore' is the original text receives support from Venantius Fortunatus (ca. 536–ca. 610): he came from Aquileia, and in his Expositio symboli 35, which is an abbreviated paraphrase of

Rufinus's treatise, wrote: 'Spiritus sanctus de Dei ore procedens et cuncta sanctificans' (for the text, see *Mon. Germ. Hist.*, Auct. 4. 1. 257). It is possible that Rufinus was recalling Ecclus. 24. 5 ('Ego ex ore Altissimi prodivi'), although this text was more usually interpreted as referring to the Son (cf. St. Augustine, *De trin.* 4. 28: PL 42. 908).

[218] For a similar argument for the full divinity of the Holy Spirit based on the co-ordination of the three Persons in the creed, see St. Epiphanius, *Haer.* 74. 14. 4 ff. (GCS 37. 332): 'From the creed itself these blasphemers of the Spirit will be found to be talking nonsense. ... Right at the beginning the formulary confesses, without any denial, "We believe in one God the Father Almighty." The words "we believe" are not used absolutely, but our belief is in God "and in Our Lord Jesus Christ." Again the phrase is not used absolutely, but our belief is in God "and in the Holy Spirit." Here too the words are not used in an absolute sense, but point to one ascription of glory, one unity of Godhead, one identity of substance, three perfect Persons but one Godhead, one substance. ... All this is contained in the threefold "We believe."' See note following.

[219] Rufinus here argues that we can only legitimately speak of 'believing in' the Persons of the Godhead: as regards the mysteries of faith and created beings, we believe that they exist. Faustus of Riez (d. 490–500) developed the same idea independently, contending that to believe in God means 'to confess Him, worship Him, adore Him, deliver oneself wholly into His lordship and jurisdiction,' whereas everything in the creed that follows 'in the Holy Spirit' should properly be construed without reference to the preposition 'in' (*De Spir. Sanct.* 1. 2: CSEL 21. 103 f.). This distinction became widely accepted in the West after 400, especially in Gallican regions: cf. the pseudo-Augustinian sermon in *Missale Gallicanum Vetus* (ed. Martène 1. 97): 'Sciendum est quod ecclesiam credere, non tamen *in* ecclesiam credere, debeamus, quia ecclesia non est Deus, sed domus Dei est.' It is also noticeable that 'esse' is placed between 'sanctam' and 'ecclesiam' in the creed of the Antiphonary of Bangor (see JNDK 402). St. Augustine distinguished carefully between 'believing God' (*credere Deo*) and 'believing in God (*credere in Deum*): cf., e.g., *Enarr. in Ps.* 77. 8; *Tract. in Ioann.* 29. 6, 53. 10 (PL 36. 988; 35. 1631, 1778). Cf. the observations by J. Schrijnen-C. Mohrmann, *Studien zur Syntax der Briefe des hl. Cyprian*, in LSP 5 (1936) 128–30. In an earlier age the use of 'in' with other articles of faith as well as with the Persons of the Godhead caused no embarrassment, as can be seen from Tertullian, *De pat.* 16 (CSEL 47. 24—'qui in resurrectionem carnis et spiritus credimus'); also St. Cyprian, *Ep.* 69. 7 (CSEL 3. 2. 756)—'nam cum dicunt, Credis

in remissionem peccatorum et vitam aeternam per sanctam ecclesiam.
. . .'). For further material, consult the article by J. E. L. Oulton in
JTS 39 (1938) 239 ff. Cf. also the related studies of T. Camelot in *Rev.
des sciences phil. et théol.* 1 (1941–42) 149–55, and C. Mohrmann in
Mélanges de Joseph de Ghellinck (Gembloux 1951) 1. 277–85; also J. H.
Crehan, *Early Christian Baptism and the Creed* (London 1948) 121–27.

[220] 2 Tim. 3. 16. That Scripture (i.e. the Old Testament) was divinely
inspired was of course a dogma of the Jews: see Josephus, *C. Ap.* 1. 8;
Philo, *Quis rer. div. haer.* 1. 510; *Quod Deus sit immut.* 1. 276; *De oper.
leg.* 2. 343; *De monarch.* 2. 222. From the earliest days the Church
extended this doctrine of inspiration to the New Testament as well,
claiming that the Holy Spirit was the organ of inspiration. So St.
Theophilus of Antioch affirms that the writings of prophets and
evangelists agree 'because all the πνευματοφόροι (i.e. 'Spirit-bearers')
have spoken by one Spirit of God' (*Ad Autol.* 3. 12: Otto 8. 218).
St. Irenaeus similarly speaks of the Apostles, after they have been
clothed with the power of the Holy Spirit from on high, as being fully
assured about all things; later he describes the Gospels as, in spite of
their fourfold form, being 'held together by one Spirit' (*Adv. haer.*
3. 1. 1, 3. 11. 11: Harvey 2. 2, 2. 47). The fragment of the Muratorian
Canon says that the leading facts of Our Lord's life have been declared
in the Gospels 'by one sovereign Spirit (uno ac principali Spiritu
declarata).' Tertullian speaks of the sacred writers as having their minds
'flooded (inundatos)' with the Holy Spirit (*Apol.* 18. 2: CSEL 69. 46).
Origen gives a more elaborate account of the process of inspiration,
saying that the sacred books are not the works of men, but were written
'by inspiration of the Holy Spirit, at the will of the Father of all,
through Jesus Christ' (*De princ.* 4. 2. 2: GCS 22. 308). St. Hippolytus
writes in a similar vein, saying that the canonical writers 'received the
inspiration, or *afflatus* (ἀπόπνοιαν), of the Father's power' (*C. Noet.*
11: PG 10. 820).

[221] Previous writers who drew up canons of Holy Scripture with
which Rufinus must have been familiar included Origen (for his canon,
see Eusebius, *Hist. eccl.* 6. 25: Schwartz 245 f.), St. Cyril of Jerusalem
(cf. *Cat.* 4. 33–6); St. Athanasius (cf. his thirty-ninth Festal Letter,
belonging to the year 367: PG 26. 1436), and St. Jerome (cf. his *Prologus
galeatus* to the Vulgate, dating from 390: PL 28. 547 f.). For a discussion
of the character and importance of Rufinus's canon, see M. Stenzel,
'Der Bibelkanon des Rufin von Aquileja,' in *Biblica* 23 (1942) 43–61;
also Introd. 20–26.

[222] Rufinus appears to treat these three books as one. According to
Origen (in Eusebius, *Hist. eccl.* 6. 25: Schwartz 245), Judges and Ruth

were reckoned as one by contemporary Jews. This probably agrees with the arrangement familiar to Josephus (C. Ap. 1. 38–42), who counted 22, as opposed to the more usual Rabbinical enumeration of 24, books in the Hebrew canon. In the Jewish Bible, which is subdivided into the Law (*Torah*), the Prophets (*Nebi'im*), and the Writings (*Kethubim*), Judges stands in the first section of the Prophets (the prophetic histories: Josue, Judges, Kings). The Talmud (Bab. Baba Bathra 14) places Ruth first among the Writings, immediately before the Psalms. It was the Greek Bible which appended it to Judges, sometimes under the same title (κριταί), and sometimes under its own name.

223 Origen, in his version of the canon cited above, bears witness to the fact that the first two books of Kings (1 and 2 Samuel), and the third and fourth books, were reckoned as two books by the Jews. So St. Jerome, in his *Prologus galeatus* (PL 28. 553), speaks of 'Samuel, quem nos Regnorum primum et secundum dicimus.' This evidence is borne out by the fact that the concluding notes of the Massoretes come at the end of 2 Kings. The Septuagint translator regarded the whole work (Samuel and Kings) as a complete history of the kingdoms of Juda and Israel, and divided them into four books entitled 'Books of the Kingdoms' (βίβλοι βασιλειῶν). St. Jerome followed this example in the Vulgate, only altering the title to 'Liber Regum.'

224 The Hebrew name, *Dibre hayyamim*, means literally 'the words (or affairs) of the days,' a term used to denote an official diary, comprising minutes of events, lists of officers, etc. Its application to this book is probably explained by the fact that a large proportion of its contents, especially towards the beginning, are statistical in character. The title Paralipomena is the one used in the Septuagint: it means 'things omitted,' and was no doubt suggested by the idea that it contained many things passed over in Kings. St. Jerome was on the right track when, in his *Prologus galeatus* (PL 28. 554), he suggested the Latin description, 'Chronicon totius historiae divinae.' From this is derived the alternative English title 'Chronicles.' In the Hebrew canon Paralipomenon belongs to the Hagiographa, or Writings, and comes last of all the Old Testament books, following Ezra-Nehemiah (1 and 2 Esdras). In the Greek Bible, however, it is placed after Kings, where its position is more logical. This is the order which Melito of Sardes (see his O.T. canon in Eusebius, *Hist. eccl.* 4. 26. 14: Schwartz 164), and Origen (*loc cit.* and *In Ps.* 1 [PG 12. 1083]) recognize.

225 In the Septuagint there are two books bearing this name— Esdras A, consisting of our 1 Esdras, certain chapters of 2 Paralipomenon, and 2 Esdras or Nehemias (it is relegated in the Vulgate to an appendix, and is labelled 3 Esdras); and Esdras B, consisting of 1 and

2 Esdras combined. In the Hebrew canon 3 Esdras (Esdras A of the Septuagint) has no place, and 1 and 2 Esdras (Vulgate) count as one book. Origen and St. Cyril both note that the Jews reckon the two books of Esdras as one. It might be thought that the books which Rufinus, like them, has in mind are 1 and 2 Esdras of the Vulgate, and so commentators have often inferred (so e.g., E. F. Morison *ad loc.*). But it seems likely that both he and they are thinking of Esdras A and B of the Septuagint, to which they have observed that only one book corresponds in the Hebrew canonical list.

226 In the Hebrew Bible Esther ranks as the last of the five 'rolls' (Megilloth) included in the Hagiographa, or Writings, and was one of the latest books to gain a place in the canon. The earliest undoubted reference to it comes in Josephus (*C. Ap.* 1. 8); and, although it eventually attained high prestige, there is evidence that its admission was sharply questioned, no doubt on account of its apparently secular tone, in the first and second centuries. Christians were equally slow in accepting it, although after the synod of Carthage of 397 (see Denzinger, *Enchiridion symbolorum* [ed. 28] 92) its position was secure. Melito of Sardes (in Eusebius, *Hist. eccl.* 4. 26. 14: Schwartz 164), St. Athanasius (he placed it among the books 'which are read': cf. *Ep. heort.* 39: PG 26. 1436), and St. Gregory of Nazianzus excluded it from the canon. On the other hand, its canonicity was acknowledged by Origen, St. Cyril, St. Jerome (who put it last on his list), and St. Augustine.

227 The twelve minor prophets always counted as one book, in the Hebrew Bible and the Septuagint alike.

228 Rufinus's canon provides noteworthy evidence that about 400 A.D. all 27 books of the New Testament were recognized as canonical at Aquileia. Apart from the Catholic Epistles, the order agrees with that which the Vulgate caused to be accepted in the West. His master St. Cyril (*Cat.* 4. 36) recognized only 26 books, making no mention of the Apocalypse, no doubt because of the opposition to it which the strictures of St. Dionysius of Alexandria had aroused. St. Cyril also, like St. Athanasius after him, placed the Catholic Epistles before the Pauline.

229 The stress which Rufinus places upon the apostolic status of these writers is probably indicative of his conviction that apostolicity was the true criterion of canonicity.

230 The first instance of 'canon' (ὁ κανών) used of the officially authorized list of sacred books comes in St. Athanasius, *De decret. Nic. syn.* 18 (PG 25. 456), when he refers to the Shepherd of Hermas as 'not belonging to the canon.' That was shortly after 350; in his Festal Letter of 367 he speaks of the Scriptures as κανονιζόμενα, in opposition

to the ἀπόκρυφα, and to distinguish them from the ἀναγινωσκόμενα (i.e. 'books which are read'). The term ὁ κανών originally meant 'a straight rod.' Metaphorically it was equivalent to the Latin 'norma,' i.e. the 'rule' or 'standard' of what is best. By 'canon of Scripture' was meant the list of sacred books which were held to conform to the accepted, official standard. For further discussion and literature cf. J. P. Christopher in ACW 2. 109 n. 89; R. T. Meyer, ACW 10. 126 n. 224.

[231] The term 'ecclesiastical' applied to sacred books is not found before Rufinus, at any rate in Latin: he seems to have attempted a threefold distinction of 'canonical,' 'ecclesiastical,' and 'apocryphal' writings. Long before him Origen had distinguished between canonical books and others, such as the Wisdom of Solomon, 'which book is not held by all to be authoritative' (*De princ.* 4. 4. 6: GCS 22. 357). St. Athanasius, in his Festal Letter (PG 26. 1437), spoke of 'other books apart from these, which have not been canonized, but which the Fathers ordained to be read by candidates who desire instruction in the faith, such as the Wisdom of Solomon, Esther, Judith, Tobias, the so-called Teaching (Didache) of the Apostles, and the Shepherd.' St. Cyril, on the other hand, was insistent that only the canonical books proper should be read—'all others should be excluded as of secondary rank. Even by yourself you should not study any writings that are not publicly read in church.' For a fuller discussion, see Introd. 24 f.

[232] The title 'Ecclesiasticus' was adopted in the West at least as early as the time of St. Cyprian (*ca.* 245). See, for example, his *Test.* 3. 110–3 (CSEL 3. 1. 181). The commonly accepted explanation is that it was so designated as being the 'Church book' *par excellence* among the 'libri ecclesiastici,' and Rufinus's words have been held to support this theory. It is scarcely satisfactory, however, for it suffers from the defect of presupposing that the book was not admitted as fully canonical at the time when the title was applied to it: it also implies that Ecclesiasticus occupied a particularly prominent position among the Deutero-canonical writings. Neither of these suggestions is accurate. Hence D. De Bruyne's argument that the name was bestowed upon it on the model of Ecclesiastes deserves to be seriously considered. See his important article, 'Le prologue, le titre et la finale de l'Ecclésiastique,' in *Zeitschr. f. d. A. T. Wiss.* 47 N.F. 6 (1929) 257 ff.

[233] Though extensively used and frequently treated as authoritative in the early Church, these books required a long time to establish their place in the official canon. All three were declared canonical by the synod of Carthage (397) and by Pope Innocent I in his letter to Exuperius of Toulouse (405): see Denzinger's *Enchiridion symbolorum* (ed. 28) 92

and 96. On the other hand, in his *Prologus galeatus* (PL 28. 556 f.) St. Jerome refused to admit them. St. Athanasius made no mention of Machabees in his Festal Letter, but reckoned Tobias and Judith among the books ' which are read.' St. Cyril does not include any of them in his canon (*Cat.* 4. 35).

[234] The *Shepherd* of Hermas is an apocryphal apocalypse which long hovered on the threshold of the New Testament. According to the Muratorian Canon, Hermas was the brother of Pope Pius I: it is possible that the earlier sections of the work go back to the time of Clement of Rome, while the final redaction was carried out in the reign of Pius I (middle of second century). Cf. J. Quasten, *Patrology* 1. 92 f. M. Dibelius, in his edition of 1923, suggests the third or fourth decade of the second century. It was reckoned as Holy Scripture by St. Irenaeus (*Adv. haer.* 4. 34. 2: Harvey 2. 213), Tertullian—at any rate before his conversión to Montanism (*De orat.* 16: CSEL 20. 190)—and Origen (*De princ.* 4. 2. 4: GCS 22. 313), although the last-mentioned was aware that it was not generally used in the Church. The Muratorian Canon (*ca.* 200) declared that it ought to be read, but recognized that it was not in the canon.

[235] Both the *Didache* (chs. 1-6) and the *Epistle of Barnabas* (chs. 18-20) include a catechetical exposition of the Christian life expressed in terms of the analogy of the two ways, the one leading to salvation and life, and the other to death (=ACW 6. 15-19 and 61-64). The relations between these two versions of 'the Two Ways' have been much discussed: see R. Knopf's edition of the *Didache* (Tübingen 1920) 2 f., and H. Windisch's edition of *Ep. Barn.* (Tübingen 1920) 408 ff. The most satisfactory conclusion is that both are independent versions of an originally Jewish proselyte catechism which the early Church took over and adapted to its purposes. Has Rufinus one or other of these two works in mind, or is he thinking of a separate document entitled *The Two Ways*? The balance of probability suggests that he is referring to the *Didache*. Eusebius (*Hist. eccl.* 3. 25. 4: Schwartz 104) classifies it as one of the disputed but spurious works, but St. Athanasius (*Ep. heort.* 39: PG 26. 1436) includes it along with the *Shepherd* among the books permitted to catechumens. Its compilation probably dates to the first half of the second century (so J. Quasten, *Patrology* 1. 37: the question has been very much debated in recent years) before the emergence of Montanism. Although it completely disappeared from the patristic epoch until 1873, when the metropolitan Bryennius of Nicomedia rediscovered it, it served in the early centuries as a model for important liturgical documents and Church Orders, such as the *Didascalia*, the so-called *Egyptian Church Order*, and Book 7 of the *Apostolical Consti-*

tutions. The correct text, it should be observed, must be 'et is qui appellatur Duae Viae,' and not, as Migne presents it, 'qui appellatur . . .'

²³⁶ The question has been raised whether we are to regard 'Iudicium Petri' (better, 'secundum Petrum') as a separate work. Because of the use of 'vel' (='or'), and the assumption that Rufinus depends for his account of the canon on St. Athanasius, scholars generally have thought that it must be taken as identical, in Rufinus's mind, with the book he calls 'Two Ways'. The point is that St. Athanasius only allows two New Testament works in his category of admitted, but non-canonical, writings, the *Didache* and the *Shepherd*, and it has therefore seemed proper that Rufinus also should allow only two. A serious difficulty, however, is that it is impossible to see how he could have confused any writing concerned with St. Peter with the *Didache*, for the Apostle is nowhere mentioned in it. But the premisses of the argument are un-tenable: there is no reason to presuppose a link between Rufinus's canon and that of St. Athanasius (see Introd. 25 f.), and 'vel' in late Latin can equally well signify 'and.' The latter point was noticed by J. Fontanini (*Hist. Literar. Aquil.* 159), and is confirmed by Rufinus's usage elsewhere (cf. his translation of Eusebius, *Hist. eccl.* 3. 3). Hence we need not feel obliged to identify the two books. As a matter of fact, a *Iudicium* ascribed to St. Peter is mentioned by St. Jerome in *De vir. ill.* 1 (TU 14. 1. 7) as an apocryphal work. No doubt, like so much of the literature of the early Church, it has long since disappeared.

²³⁷ The term 'apocryphal' was originally used to designate books containing hidden teaching not to be disclosed to ordinary people. For a good example, cf. 4 Esdras 14. 45–7, where the author speaks of 70 apocalyptic writings which may be delivered only to 'the wise among your people.' A second stage in its history is reflected in its application by certain Fathers to books which may be read in private for edifica-tion, as opposed to being read in public at the Church's services. For this, cf. Origen, *In Matt.* 10. 18 (GCS 40. 1. 24). Finally, the word came to bear the sense of 'false,' 'spurious,' 'heretical.' This is the sense it has in St. Cyril, *Cat.* 4. 35, and also here.

²³⁸ 'Holy Church' was a very ancient credal article, its earliest appearance being in the formula contained in the second-century *Epistula apostolorum*—see C. Schmidt, *Gespräche Jesu mit seinen Jüngern nach seiner Auferstehung*, TU 43 (1919) 32—and in the baptismal questions implied by Tertullian in *De bapt.* 6 (CSEL 20. 206). St. Cyril's creed added the epithet 'Catholic,' a term which he explains at length in *Cat.* 18. 23. It did not appear as a description of the Church in the Old Roman creed, and the first Western formula to embody it is that of

Niceta of Remesiana (*ca.* 335–*ca.* 414). Later it became a favourite item in Spanish and Gallican creeds. See JNDK 384 ff.

²³⁹ An echo of Eph. 5. 27: '. . . gloriosam ecclesiam, non habentem maculam aut rugam aut aliquid huiusmodi.'

²⁴⁰ St. Cyril also emphasizes (*Cat.* 18. 26) the danger of confusing the numerous heretical congregations with the one Catholic Church, although he singles out only the Marcionites and the Manichees for mention. An account of most of the heretics named here, as of their opinions, will be found in the following notes. Valentinus, whose ideas Rufinus omits to summarize below, was the most influential of second-century Gnostic theologians: for a full discussion, see F. Sagnard, *La gnose Valentinienne* (Paris 1947). Born in Egypt (so St. Epiphanius, *Haer.* 31. 2. 3: GCS 25. 384), he taught in Rome *ca.* 136–65, and there separated himself from the Church: according to St. Epiphanius (*Haer.* 31. 7. 2: GCS 25. 396), he retired to Cyprus, where he died. His teaching is not easy to distinguish from that of his followers, but its leading features were its dualism and its elaborate doctrine of aeons. Thirty in number, and arranged in pairs deriving from the unoriginate Father, these aeons constituted the divine world, or Pleroma, and alongside them a place was found for Christ and the Holy Spirit, and also the Cross (see St. Hippolytus, *Ref. omn. haer.* 6. 30. 6, 31. 6: GCS 26. 157 f., 159). The system, though Gnostic through and through, was deeply coloured with Christian ideas, and was in fact a Christian heresy. What made the propaganda of the Valentinians particularly dangerous was their skill in representing themselves as orthodox: cf. St. Irenaeus, *Adv. haer.* 3. 15. 2 (Harvey 2. 79–81); Tertullian, *Adv. Valent.* 1 (CSEL 47. 157 f.).

²⁴¹ Ps. 25. 5. The Vulgate reads 'odivi' for Rufinus's 'odi.' St. Cyril quotes the text (*Cat.* 18.25), but in reference to the rejected Church of Judaism.

²⁴² Cant. 6. 8. The quotation is incomplete: cf. the Vulgate: 'Una est columba mea, perfecta mea, una est matris suae, electa genetrici suae.'

²⁴³ An echo of Ps. 25. 4.

²⁴⁴ For Marcion, see A. von Harnack, *Marcion: Das Evangelium vom fremden Gott* (4. ed. Leipzig 1924); E. C. Blackman, *Marcion and his Influence* (London 1948). Born at Sinope, in Pontus, he came to Rome about 140: he was excommunicated in 144, and died about 160. The distinctive feature of his teaching was the absolute line of demarcation he drew between the Old and the New Testaments, and so between Judaism and Christianity. This led him to reject the whole Old Testament, and to admit into his Scriptural canon only St. Luke's Gospel

and the first ten Pauline epistles: even these he expunged of all seemingly pro-Jewish traits. In his view the God revealed in the Old Testament was the creator of the world and man, and was a cruel tyrant demanding obedience, sacrifices, and legal works, whereas the God revealed by Jesus is merciful and loving, asking only faith. Marcion established an opposition church, with a ministry, and a closely-knit organization modelled on those of the Catholic Church, which remained vigorous as late as the fourth century.

²⁴⁵ For the Ebionites, see St. Irenaeus, *Adv. haer.* I. 22 (Harvey I. 212 f.); Tertullian, *De praescr. haer.* 33 (CSEL 70. 41); Origen, *C. Cels.* 2. 1, 5. 61, 5. 65 (GCS 2. 126 f., 3. 65, 68=Chadwick 66, 311 f., 314); St. Epiphanius, *Haer.* 30. 17 (GCS 25. 355 ff.). They seem to have been the descendants of the Judaizing Christians whom St. Paul combated in his Epistles to the Galatians and the Romans. They required strict observance of the Law (circumcision, etc.), and accepted Jesus simply as Messiah, denying His divinity and His supernatural conception (so St. Irenaeus, *Adv. haer.* 5. I. 3: Harvey 2. 316 f.; but cf. Origen, *C. Cels.* 5. 61: GCS 3. 65=Chadwick 311 f.). It was Tertullian, apparently, who invented an eponymous heresiarch, Ebion, to account for their name (*loc. cit.*): it is unlikely that such a person ever existed. The term 'Ebionites' simply means 'the poor,' and reflects the honourable title claimed by the primitive Jerusalem community (Rom. 15. 26; Gal. 2. 10). Cf. K. Holl, *Gesammelte Aufsätze zur Kirchengeschichte* (Tübingen 1928) 2. 58 f.

²⁴⁶ For a full account of Manichaeism, see F. C. Burkitt, *The Religion of the Manichees* (Cambridge 1924), and the important article by G. Bardy, 'Manichéisme,' DTC 9. 2 (1927) 1841-95: also H. Ch. Puech, *Le Manichéisme, son fondateur, sa doctrine* (Paris 1949). Its founder, Mani, was a native of Seleucia-Ctesiphon (in Babylon), and began to preach in Persia in 241/2: he was executed on the orders of the emperor Bahram I in 276/7. His followers, as Rufinus notes, formed a 'church,' well organized and with a hierarchy of officials, and this constituted one of the most formidable rivals of Christianity. His teaching, with its attempt to solve the problem of evil by a doctrine of dualism (Light and Darkness), included a denial of the birth and real passion of Jesus, and the claim that he was himself the apostle of Jesus and the Paraclete whose coming He had foretold. He seems to have been influenced by Marcion, and may have borrowed his attitude to the Old Testament from him. It is not certain that Rufinus is correct in attributing to him a theory of metempsychosis: what he seems to have taught was that anyone who in this life failed to qualify as one of the *electi* had to undergo a severe process of purification, tied to the world of matter,

after death. Modern research, as represented by such scholars as F. C. Burkitt, inclines to endorse Rufinus's assumption that Manichaeism, so far from adopting Christian elements for propagandist reasons, was really a Christian heresy. To some extent this explains how such a great thinker as St. Augustine was able to remain 'nine whole years' (373–82: *De mor. Manich.* 19—PL 33. 1374) as an *auditor* of the sect. Having been put off, as he admits, by the crude style and obscurity of the Bible, he found himself attracted by the Manichaeans' claims to know the truth, their materialistic conception of God, their explanation of evil, and their apparent asceticism (cf. esp. *Confess.* 3. 5–10: CSEL 33. 1. 50–60).

[247] Paul of Samosata, who became bishop of Antioch in 260 and was condemned at the council held there in 268, counted as the classic heretic of the third century. For a full discussion of his views, which are not easy to disentangle precisely, see F. Loofs, *Paulus von Samosata* (Leipzig 1924), and G. Bardy, *Paul de Samosate* (2. ed. Louvain 1929); cf. also G. L. Prestige, *God in Patristic Thought* (London 1952) 115 f., 201–209. According to the most plausible interpretation of his teaching (cf. e.g. Ps.–Leontius, *De sect.* 3. 3: PG 86. 1213 ff.), he held that the Father alone exists substantially: the Word is no more than His spoken utterance, and hence is not a separate hypostasis. As regards Christology, he taught that the existence of Jesus Christ, the Son of God, began with His conception by the Holy Spirit of the Virgin Mary; He was distinct from the eternal Word who indwelt Him, and He only attained to divine status through progressive advancement.—For the career of Photinus, see n. 5 above. Strictly speaking, he was a disciple of Marcellus of Ancyra, carrying to extremes the modalist strain in his master's thought. At the same time, he had adoptionist leanings, teaching that Christ was a man like other men except in His miraculous conception, and that His elevation to the divine level was the result of His moral perfection. For this reason he was very commonly, though inexactly, classified with Paul.

[248] Along with Aetius, Eunomius was the leader of that extremist form of Arianism ('Anomoeism') which emerged in the fifties of the fourth century teaching that the Son is a creature and utterly unlike the Father. It found expression in the formula ('the Blasphemy') ratified by the second council of Sirmium (357). In one respect his system differed from that of Arius himself (280–336): whereas Arius held that the Son was promoted to the divine status and name as a reward for His virtues, Eunomius was prepared to agree that He enjoyed these from the very beginning of His existence. As regards the Holy Spirit, the teaching of Arius himself was not explicitly formulated: there are

hints in St. Athanasius (*C. Ar.* 1. 6; *De syn.* 15: PG 26. 24; 708) that he thought of Him as differing in substance from the Father and the Son. For the later Arians, and for Eunomius himself, there was no doubt that the Spirit was a creature, the work of the Son: cf. Eunomius, *Apol.* 28 (PG 30. 868); St. Basil, *Adv. Eunom.* 2. 33 (PG 29. 649). The word *mittendarius* which Rufinus uses to express their depreciatory attitude to the Holy Spirit designated an officer attached to the imperial palace who was sent by the emperor as the bearer of his orders, especially on business connected with the collection of taxes. Cf. its use in *Codex Theodosianus* 6. 30. 2.

[249] Rufinus is alluding to the right-wing Pneumatomachians. As early as 359 St. Athanasius, in his correspondence with bishop Serapion of Thmuis, was called upon to refute a sect, the Tropici, who 'have separated themselves from Arianism because of its blasphemous estimate of the Son, but entertain wrong-headed ideas about the Holy Spirit, maintaining that He is not only a creature, but one of the ministering spirits, differing from the angels only in degree' (*Ad Serap.* 1. 1: PG 26. 532). On the eve of the council of Constantinople (381), we find the more moderate Macedonians taking a similar line, accepting the consubstantiality of the Son, but refusing to acknowledge the Spirit as divine: cf., e.g., St. Gregory of Nazianzus, *Orat. theol.* 5. 5, 5. 24; *Orat.* 41. 8 (PG 36. 137, 160, 440). The full homoousion of the Spirit was established by the council, and after 383 Theodosius proscribed Macedonianism with a series of severe edicts. For the Tropici and the Macedonian heresy, see C. R. B. Shapland, *The letters of Saint Athanasius concerning the Holy Spirit* (London 1951) 18–34.

[250] Matt. 28. 19. Rufinus uses an abbreviated text. St. Cyril (*Cat.* 16. 4) cites the verse as showing that the Holy Spirit must be honoured along with the Father and the Son in the one Godhead. Cf. the frequent appeal to the text by St. Basil in *De Spir. sanct.* In the following sentence Rufinus echoes Matt. 19. 6 (Mark 10. 9).

[251] Rufinus refers to the heresy of Apollinarius (*ca.* 310–*ca.* 390). At first the friend of St. Athanasius and a champion of the Nicene faith, he developed the view that the Logos took the place of the rational soul, or νοῦς, as distinct from the animal soul, or ψυχή, in Jesus Christ. According to this conception of human nature, the former was the intellectual and volitional principle in a man, and the latter the life principle: an animal or plant might have a ψυχή because it was alive. His argument was that, if the Saviour had possessed a rational soul, both the unity of His person and His sinlessness would have been imperilled. His teaching, involving as it did a denial of the completeness of the incarnation, was condemned by the council of Alexandria in 362, by

synods held at Rome in 374, 376, and 380, and by the council of Constantinople in 381. The best account of it is given by A. Grillmeier in
Das Konzil von Chalkedon (Würzburg 1951) 1. 102–117.

²⁵² The powerful Donatist schism, named after one of its leaders,
bishop Donatus of Casae Nigrae, sprang up in North Africa as a result
of squabbles over the succession of Mensurius, bishop of Carthage, who
died in 311. A fanatical opposition party, headed by an influential
widow Lucilla, declared the election of the orthodox nominee,
Caecilian, invalid on the ground that one of his consecrators, Felix of
Aptunga, had been a *traditor*, i.e. had surrendered the Scriptures to the
authorities during the persecution of Diocletian. In spite of a series of
decisions in Caecilian's favour (at Rome in 313, Arles in 314, Milan in
316), the sect spread apace and ravaged the Church of Africa, and in
the early years of the fifth century the most drastic measures were taken
against it by the secular power. It was nourished by two erroneous ideas
which had held sway over North African Christians since the middle of
the third century, the Novatianist theory (see below) that membership
of the Church was confined to the righteous, and the Cyprianic doctrine
that the validity of sacraments depended on the worth of the minister.

²⁵³ Novatus was the leader of the group of clergy who in 249
opposed the election of St. Cyprian as bishop of Carthage, and later
organized a schism against him on the ground of his alleged severity
towards Christians who had lapsed in the Decian persecution. The
sectarians whom Rufinus envisages here, however, are the Novatianists, named after Novatian, the Roman theologian and contemporary
of St. Cyprian, who instigated a much more serious schism against
Pope Cornelius. Novatian espoused the cause of rigorism, accusing
Cornelius of undue lenience in regard to churchmen who had aposta-
tized during the persecution: he himself wanted to withhold all
ecclesiastical pardon, until their deathbed, from apostates of every
category. Novatus, excommunicated at Carthage, joined forces with
Novatian, swinging over from a policy of laxity to one of rigour, and
the names of the two heretics were often confused. The Novatianist
sect spread far and wide, and had a long history: cf. E. Amann,
'Novatien et novatianism,' DTC 11. 1 (1931) 815–49. Its members were
distinguished by an extreme puritanism, and indeed called themselves
'Cathari,' or 'the pure' (cf. St. Epiphanius, *Haer.* 59. 1. 1: GCS 2. 363).
Novatian himself, so far as can be judged, showed no hostility to
second marriages, and certain groups of the later Novatianists, particularly in the West, countenanced them. But there is evidence which
suggests, in confirmation of what Rufinus says in this passage, that in
the East at any rate they were inclined to view second marriages with

suspicion: cf. St. Epiphanius, *Haer.* 59. 3 (GCS 31. 366); Socrates, *Hist. Eccl.* 5. 22 (PG 67. 641).

[254] Rufinus here pointedly castigates errors currently attributed to Origen, for supporting whose doctrines he had himself been subjected to sharp criticism from St. Jerome. His contemptuous 'if indeed such are to be found' deserves notice: modern authorities (e.g. F. Cavallera, *Saint Jérôme, sa vie et son oeuvre* [Paris 1922] 1. 204) would agree that few, if any, of his contemporaries were guilty of them. (a) The idea that the Son's vision and knowledge of the Father are defective was characteristic of Arianism in its original form, but Origen was accused of having sponsored it: cf. St. Epiphanius, *Haer.* 64. 4. 3 (GCS 31. 410); St. Jerome, *Ep.* 124. 13 (CSEL 56. 115); *C. Ioann. Hier.* 7 (PL 23. 360). Actually, Origen distinguished between *seeing* the Father (which he held to be impossible for the Son, since sight demands a physical eye) and knowing Him: cf. *De princ.* 1. 1. 8 (GCS 22. 25 f.). But on occasion his language lends colour to the charge, as in *De princ.* 4. 4. 8 (35) (GCS 22. 358 ff.)—a passage preserved by Justinian, *Ep. ad Menn.* (Mansi 9. 525). (b) The belief that the Son's reign has a limited duration, a heresy normally associated with Marcellus of Ancyra (see n. 204 above), was also laid at the door of Origen: cf. the synodal letter (400 A.D.) of Theophilus of Alexandria (translated by St. Jerome, *Ep.* 92. 2: CSEL 55. 149), and the twelfth of the fifteen anathemas ascribed to the Fifth General Council (553 A.D.), but probably emanating from a σύνοδος ἐνδημοῦσα held at Constantinople in 543 (cf. Hefele-Leclercq 2. 2. 1187 ff., which gives the text). (c) Correctly understood, Origen's teaching about the resurrection, while insisting on the spiritual nature of the resurrection body, did not deny its essential identity with the mortal body. Yet this particular doctrine of his was consistently misrepresented and attacked. For example, Methodius of Olympus (✠311) was early in the field with criticisms (cf. e.g. the fragments in his *De resurrectione* 3. 3 ff.: GCS 27. 391 ff.), and the polemical writings of St. Epiphanius and St. Jerome abound with them. Rufinus states his own undoubtedly orthodox position in several passages, e.g. *Apol. ad Anast.* 4; *Apol.* 1. 6–9 (PL 21. 625; 545–7). Towards the end of the section under discussion we notice his emphatic declaration that Christ 'rose again from the dead in the identical flesh with which He was born.' (d) Another widely criticized Origenist doctrine was that of the *apocatastasis*, or restitution of all things, according to which all rational creatures will in the end be restored to friendship and unity with God. This was the solution Origen proposed for the problem of evil, and in harmony with it he taught that the function of divine punishment was educative. For a full

treatment of it, see J. Daniélou, *Origène* (Paris 1948) 271 ff.; C. Lenz, 'Apokatastasis,' *Reallex. f. Ant. u. Christ.* 1 (1950) 510–516; H. Graef, ACW 18. 189 n. 89. Involved in his theory was the implication that the sufferings of the damned, including the Devil himself, would not be everlasting, but that even the most evil beings would ultimately be reconciled to God. Sometimes Origen himself was hesitant on the point, as in his *Comm. in Ep. ad Rom.* 8. 9 (PG 14. 1185), where he suggests that Lucifer will not be converted even 'in fine saeculi': but his general teaching inevitably points to this conclusion. This struck the orthodox as contradicting the righteousness of God's judgment, and thus was always one of the most hotly contested features of his system. For example, cf. Theophilus of Alexandria's synodal letter: St. Jerome, *Ep.* 92. 1 (CSEL 55. 147 f.); St. Jerome, *C. Ioann. Hier.* 7 (PL 23. 360); etc.

255 The clause 'Forgiveness of sins' was part of the Church's most ancient creed material. Although it did not stand among the baptismal interrogations in St. Hippolytus's *Tradition*, Tertullian's language in *De bapt.* 11 (CSEL 20. 210) indicates that he was familiar with it as a credal question. The five-clause summary quoted by the second-century *Epistula apostolorum* (text in C. Schmidt, *Gespräche Jesu* 32: also JNDK 82), also included a mention of it. Originally the clause referred to the remission of sins imparted by baptism, as is brought out in the form of words preferred by Eastern creeds; cf. ἐν βάπτισμα μετανοίας εἰς ἄφεσιν ἁμαρτιῶν (i.e. 'one baptism of repentance unto the remission of sins'), in the creed of Jerusalem. Gradually its meaning was extended to cover the forgiveness obtained through confession and absolution. Cf. St. Augustine, *Serm.* 213. 8 (PL 38. 1064). On the subject, see JNDK 160–63, 384.

256 Pagan criticisms of the Christian doctrine of forgiveness go back at least as far as Celsus. He argued (cf. Origen, *C. Cels.* 3. 65: GCS 2. 258 f.=Chadwick 172) that 'it is manifest to everyone that no one by chastisement, much less by merciful treatment, could effect a complete change in those who are sinners both by nature and custom: for it is extremely hard to change a man's nature.' Similarly Porphyry considers adult baptism immoral, seeing that it claims to abolish so many stains of sin by a single immersion and by the mere invocation of Christ's name (frag. 88). Cf. the emperor Julian, in his *Symposium* 336 A, B, for a similar argument (date 362).

257 Rufinus's doctrine is that, since the seat of moral evil is the will, evil can only be eradicated by an alteration in the bias of the will. His sharp distinction between the external act and the interior state motivating it deserves note. Origen, dealing with analogous objections

advanced by Celsus, had also stressed the importance of the transformation of the will (*C. Cels.* 3. 69: GCS 2. 261 f. = Chadwick 174 f.). St. Cyril speaks of sin as 'an offspring of the will' (*Cat.* 2. 1), and goes on to argue: 'Sin then is, as we have said, a fearful evil, but not incurable: fearful for him who clings to it, but cured easily in the case of the man who puts it from him by repentance.'

[258] Cf. St. Jerome's words in *C. Ioann. Hier.* 28 (PL 23. 380): 'In symbolo fidei et spei nostrae . . . post confessionem Trinitatis et unitatem ecclesiae omne Christiani dogmatis sacramentum carnis resurrectione concluditur.' Eastern creeds, e.g. that of Jerusalem commented on by St. Cyril, early included a reference to LIFE EVERLASTING, but Western creeds were slower in incorporating it. The earliest appearance of such a clause is in the Balkan creed of Niceta of Remesiana and the North African creeds quoted by St. Augustine. On the question, see JNDK 175 f. and 386 f. RESURRECTION OF THE FLESH featured from very early times in the Church's creed material: cf., e.g., Tertullian, *De virg. vel.* 1 (Oehler 1. 884), and St. Hippolytus, *Apostolic Tradition* 21 (G. Dix 37). The form preferred by the New Testament and by a number of patristic authors was 'resurrection of the dead': the choice of 'flesh' was probably dictated by the desire to counter anti-realist interpretations of the doctrine of the resurrection —see n. 268 below. In the form current at Aquileia, as we shall shortly see, FLESH had THIS prefixed to it.

[259] The resurrection of the body could have no place in the system of the Gnostic Valentinus. He held a docetic view of Christ, regarding His body as mere appearance, and he taught that man's redemption consists in the liberation of the spiritual element planted secretly in his soul by Achamoth from its material trammels. Cf. Ps.-Tertullian, *Adv. omn. haer.* 4 (Oehler 2. 759 ff.); St. Irenaeus, *Adv. haer.* 1. 1. 11 (Harvey 1. 51 ff.); St. Epiphanius, *Haer.* 31. 7. 6 (GCS 25. 396: τὴν δὲ τῶν νεκρῶν ἀνάστασιν ἀπαρνοῦνται). For the Manichaean denial of the resurrection, see ch. 39 above. Any idea of a physical resurrection was excluded by the radical dualism of the Manichaean system.

[260] Isa. 26. 19. The Old Latin follows the Septuagint. Cf. the Vulgate: 'Vivent mortui tui, interfecti mei resurgent.'

[261] Dan. 12. 2. Again the Old Latin reflects the Septuagint (Theodotion's version).

[262] Mark. 12. 26 f.; Matt. 22. 31 f. Rufinus seems to conflate the two passages in his memory.

[263] Matt. 22. 30.

[264] This anti-Christian argument is borrowed from St. Cyril, *Cat.* 18. 2.

[265] I Cor. 15. 36–8. The Vulgate has minor variations, inserting 'as' ('ut puta') before 'of wheat,' reading 'some of the rest' for 'some other kinds of wheat,' and substituting 'sicut' for 'prout.'

[266] For the argument, cf. St. Cyril, *Cat.* 4. 30: 'Will He who raises the wheat, which is sown every year on our behalf and which dies, have any difficulty in raising us, on whose behalf that same wheat is raised?' St. Cyril also, in *Cat.* 18. 3, makes a similar appeal to God's omnipotence.

[267] This illustration is also borrowed from St. Cyril, *Cat.* 18. 3.

[268] The addition of THIS before FLESH is peculiar to the Aquileian creed. Rufinus again refers to the addition in *Apol.* 1. 5 and 9 (PL 21. 544 and 547). He interprets it as certifying the identity of the resurrection body with the historical body. We recall that among the Origenist errors attributed to him was the belief that, while the body would rise again, the flesh as such would not. Cf. St. Jerome, *Ep.* 84. 5 (CSEL 55. 126): 'Credimus, inquiunt, resurrectionem futuram corporum. Hoc si bene dicatur, pura confessio est. Sed quia corpora sunt coelestia et terrestria, et aer iste et aura tenuis iuxta naturam suam corpora nominentur, corpus ponunt, non carnem, ut orthodoxus corpus audiens carnem putet, haereticus spiritum recognoscat.' Rufinus's discussion of the resurrection here and elsewhere reveals no trace of unorthodoxy. Cf. *Apol.* 1. 4 (PL 21. 544): '. . . so that we believe that our resurrection will be in the same manner and process, and in the same form, as the resurrection of Our Lord Himself from the dead: that the bodies we shall receive will not be phantoms or thin vapours, as some slanderously affirm that we say, but these very bodies of ours in which we live and in which we die. For how can we truly believe in the resurrection of the flesh, unless the very nature of the flesh remains in it truly and substantially? It is then without any equivocation that we confess the resurrection of this real and substantial flesh of ours in which we live.' Cf. also the following sections, especially 9 (PL 21. 547): 'I have made a lengthier answer than I intended on this single article of the resurrection, through fear lest through being too brief I should lay myself open to fresh aspersions. Consequently, I have made mention not only of the body, as to which cavils are raised, but of the flesh: and not only of the flesh, but I have added "this flesh." Further, I have spoken not only of "this flesh", but of "this natural flesh." I have not even stopped here, but have asserted that not even the completeness of the several members will be lacking. I have only demanded that, in harmony with the Apostle's words, it should rise incorruptible instead of corruptible, glorious instead of dishonoured, immortal instead of frail, spiritual instead of natural; and that we should

think of the members of the spiritual body as being without taint of corruption or frailty.'

²⁶⁹ The practice of signing oneself with the cross sprang up remarkably early. Cf. Tertullian's statement in *De cor. mil.* 3 (CSEL 70. 158— dated 211): 'Ad omnem progressum atque promotum, ad omnem aditum et exitum, ad calciatum, ad vestitum, ad lavacra, ad mensas, ad lumina, ad cubilia, ad sedilia, quacunque nos conversatio exercet, frontem crucis signaculo terimus.' Origen similarly describes Christians (*Sel. in Ezech.* 9: PG 13. 800 f.) as marking their foreheads with the Greek letter *tau*, i.e. the cross, whenever they take any task in hand, and particularly when beginning their prayers or their reading of Scripture. Another early witness is St. Cyprian, *De laps.* 2; *Ep.* 58. 9 (CSEL 3. 1. 238; 3. 2. 664). Cf. St. Cyril, *Cat.* 4. 14, 13. 36; and for another reference in Rufinus, see his *Apol.* 1. 5 (PL 21. 544). St. Jerome lays it down (*Ep.* 22. 37: CSEL 54. 202) for virgins that 'in everything we do, in every step we take, let our hand trace the sign of the Lord's cross'; see also *Ep.* 130. 9 (CSEL 56. 188—'. . . mark your brow frequently with the sign of the cross, lest the Destroyer of Egypt find a place in you'). In ancient times, as these texts imply, the practice was for Christians to sign their brows with the hand, probably the thumb. Experts trace the modern fashion of crossing oneself, from brow to breast, and then from left shoulder to right, to the eighth century: see A. A. Pelliccia, *De Christianae Ecclesiae primae, mediae et novissimae aetatis politia* (Vercelli 1780) ch. 4. 194. It was also customary, in the early centuries, to make the sign of the cross over an object, e.g. a bed (Tertullian, *Ad ux.* 2. 5: CSEL 70. 118=ACW 13. 30), or a bowl of water (St. Epiphanius, *Haer.* 30. 12: GCS 25. 348), or to trace it in the air as a protective gesture (cf. Sozomen, *Hist. Eccl.* 7. 26: PG 67. 1500). Cf. H. Leclercq, 'Signe de la Croix,' DACL 3. 2 (1914) 3139–44; W. P. Le Saint, ACW 13. 129 n. 116.

²⁷⁰ 1 Cor. 15. 13 f. The Vulgate differs in details, the most important being the reading 'inanis est et fides vestra' instead of Rufinus's 'vacua est et fides nostra.'

²⁷¹ *Ibid.* 15. 20–24. Again the Vulgate exhibits minor variations, reading 'primitiae' (='first fruits') on both occasions where Rufinus has 'initium,' and 'deinde ii qui sunt Christi, qui in adventu eius crediderunt' in place of his 'deinde hi qui sunt Christi in adventu eius.'

²⁷² *Ibid.* 15. 51 f. The Vulgate has 'sed non omnes immutabimur' for Rufinus's 'non omnes autem immutabimur.' This is the Western text, and is represented by D (Codex Bezae), the Old Latin versions, etc., and it differs radically from what is accepted as the authentic text, viz. 'We shall not all sleep, but we shall all be changed.' The latter has the

support of B (Codex Vaticanus), the Sahidic and Bohairic versions, and indeed the majority of Greek MSS. The alternative form known to Rufinus ('We shall all sleep, but we shall not all be changed') has the authority of Codex Sinaiticus. St. Jerome discusses the Pauline text in *Ep.* 119. 2 ff. (CSEL 55. 447 ff.).

²⁷³ 1 Thess. 4. 12–16. In v. 12 the Vulgate correctly reads 'nolumus' for Rufinus's 'nolo.' In v. 14 it reads, again correctly, 'qui residui sumus in adventum Domini' in place of his 'qui reliqui sumus in adventu Domini.' There are other minor differences.

²⁷⁴ Ezech. 37. 12. The Vulgate substitutes 'tumulos vestros' for 'sepulchra vestra' of the Old Latin. The text is quoted by St. Cyril, *Cat.* 18. 15, as a proof of resurrection.

²⁷⁵ Job 14. 7–10. Cf. the Vulgate: 'Lignum habet spem; si praecisum fuerit, rursum virescit, et rami eius pullulant. 8. Si senuerit in terra radix eius, et in pulvere emortuus fuerit truncus illius, 9. ad odorem aquae germinabit et faciet comam, quasi cum primum plantatum est. 10. Homo vero, cum mortuus fuerit, et nudatus, atque consumptus, ubi, quaeso, est?' Rufinus's Old Latin closely follows the Septuagint, with the difference that in the latter the final sentence is not interrogative. In the original Job is urging the hopelessness of any life after death. Rufinus borrows the text, and the argument for a resurrection which he builds upon it, from St. Cyril, *Cat.* 18. 15, who likewise attempts to justify the interrogative form: 'As it were remonstrating and reproving (for thus ought we to read the words *is he no more?* with an interrogation), Job says, since a tree falls and revives, shall not man, for whom all trees were made, himself revive?'

²⁷⁶ *Ibid.* 14. 14. The Vulgate has: 'Putasne, mortuus homo rursum vivat?' This correctly represents the original Hebrew: the point of it is that the suggestion of a future life is too good to be true. The Septuagint, however, omits the point of interrogation and reads ζήσεται. This would seem to be 'probably a dogmatic rendering, intended to make Job affirm distinctly the thought of the resurrection' (Driver and Gray, *International Critical Commentary* 92). The omission of the question mark precisely reverses the meaning. St. Cyril, whom Rufinus is again copying, quotes the verse in this form in *Cat.* 18. 15: 'And that thou mayest not suppose that I am forcing the words, read what follows. For after saying by way of question, *When mortal man falls, is he no more?* he says, *For if a man die, he shall live again;* and immediately he adds, *I will wait till I be made again;* and again elsewhere, *Who shall raise up on the earth my skin, which endures these things?*'

²⁷⁷ *Ibid.* 14. 14: the continuation of the passage discussed above. The original runs: 'All the days of my warfare would I wait, till my release

should come', which correctly appears in the Vulgate as: 'Cunctis diebus quibus milito, expecto donec veniat immutatio mea.' In the preceding verses Job has been strenuously denying that a man can be awakened from the sleep of death. In vv. 13 ff. his mind plays yearningly with the hope that it might be otherwise, although the possibility seems too good to be true. In this verse he is saying that, if only this were the way God ordered things, he would be content to await in Sheol until His wrath had passed over and He were ready to receive him again into communion. In all this there is of course no explicit affirmation of a life after death, much less of a resurrection. But the Septuagint reads ἕως ἂν πάλιν γένωμαι (='until I come into being again'). This enabled St. Cyril (see preceding note), and basing himself on him Rufinus, to interpret the passage as clearly pointing to a resurrection.

²⁷⁸ *Ibid.* 19. 25 f. The original is one of the most difficult and disputed passages in the Old Testament: the text is probably corrupt. An approximation to a translation would run: ('I am sure that my Goel, or vindicator, liveth), and that he will stand up at the last upon the earth; 26. and after this my skin has been destroyed, yet outside my body shall I see God.' The Vulgate renders it: '(Scio enim quod Redemptor meus vivit), et in novissimo die de terra surrecturus sum; 26. et rursum circumdabor pelle mea, (et in carne mea videbo Deum).' St. Cyril (*Cat.* 18. 15), and in dependence on him Rufinus, use the Septuagint text.

²⁷⁹ For Rufinus's ideas about the nature of the resurrection body, see n. 268 above, and *Apol.* 1. 5–9 (PL 21. 544–47). Cf. also the summary statement in *Apol. ad Anast.* 4 (PL 21. 625): 'Sed et carnis nostrae resurrectionem fatemur integre et perfecte futuram: huius ipsius carnis in qua nunc vivimus. Non, ut quidam calumniantur, alteram pro hac resurrecturam dicimus, sed hanc ipsam, nullo omnino eius membro amputato vel aliqua corporis parte desecta, sed cui nihil omnino ex omni natura sua desit, nisi sola corruptio.'

²⁸⁰ 1 Cor. 15. 53: he quotes the same text in *Apol.* 1. 7 (PL 21. 546). The Vulgate agrees.

²⁸¹ St. Augustine gives expression to precisely the same thought in *De fide et symb.* 23 (CSEL 41. 30): 'Haec ergo visibilis, quae proprie dicitur caro, sine dubitatione credenda est resurgere. Videtur enim Paulus apostolus eam tanquam digito ostendere cum dicit, *Oportet corruptibile hoc induere incorruptionem.* Cum enim dicit, *hoc,* in eam quasi digitum intendit. Quod autem visible est, id potest digito ostendi. . . . Et *mortale hoc induere immortalitatem* cum legitur, eadem significatur visibilis caro, quia in eam identidem velut digitus intenditur.'

[282] Rom. 6. 9. The Vulgate has minor variations.

[283] I.e. ch. 43, where he also cites 1 Thess. 4. 16.

[284] Phil. 3. 21. Cf. the reading of the Vulgate: 'Qui reformabit corpus humilitatis nostrae, configuratum corpori claritatis suae,' which is closer to the original Greek. In *Apol.* 1. 6 f. (PL 21. 545) Rufinus argues that Christ's resurrection body provides the model and pattern of our own. Cf. esp. 6: 'Since then Christ has given His own resurrection as a typical instance, . . . can anyone be so mad as to imagine that he himself will rise again in a fashion different from Him who first opened the gate of resurrection?' and 7: 'Since then, in reference to our hope of resurrection, Christ is set forth all through as the archtype. . . .'

[285] Eph. 2. 6. Some MSS read 'coexcitavit' for 'consuscitavit.' The Vulgate differs: 'et conresuscitavit, et consedere fecit in caelestibus in Christo Iesu.'

[286] This seems to be a conflation of Matt. 13. 43 ('Tunc iusti fulgebunt sicut sol in regno Patris eorum') and Dan. 12. 3 ('Qui autem docti fuerint, fulgebunt quasi splendor firmamenti'). Cf. Wisdom 3. 7: 'Fulgebunt iusti, et tanquam scintillae in arundineto discurrent.'

[287] 1 Cor. 15. 44.

[288] According to Gen. 2. 7, 'Formavit igitur Dominus Deus hominem de limo terrae.' Rufinus's desire to show that the great truths of revelation are in harmony with the natural reason is noticeable. We recall his analogous treatment of, for example, the remission of sins in ch. 40.

[289] Dan. 12. 2. It is a loose quotation, but, as in ch. 41, reflects the Septuagint (Theodotion's version). Cf. the Vulgate: 'Et multi de his qui dormiunt in terrae pulvere evigilabunt, alii in vitam aeternam, et alii in opprobrium ut videant semper.'

[290] Cf. Rufinus's words in ch. 35: 'Ut ergo fiat distinctio personarum, affectionis vocabula secernuntur, quibus ille Pater intelligatur ex quo omnia, et quia ipse non habeat patrem; iste Filius, tanquam qui ex Patre natus est; et hic Spiritus Sanctus, tanquam de utroque procedens et cuncta sanctificans.'

[291] Cf. his remark in ch. 40 at the close of his discussion of the remission of sins: 'Hoc modo fides nostra non invenitur naturalibus rationibus adversari.' The point of 'divinae libertati' seems to be that pagan critics used arguments derived apparently from common sense, or natural reason, to throw doubt on God's freedom to forgive sins. See nn. 256 and 257 above.

INDEX

INDEX

ANCIENT CHRISTIAN WRITERS

The Works of the Fathers in Translation

Edited by

J. QUASTEN, S.T.D., and J. C. PLUMPE, Ph.D.

1. THE EPISTLES OF ST. CLEMENT OF ROME AND ST. IGNATIUS OF ANTIOCH. Trans. by James A. Kleist, S.J., Ph.D. Pages x + 162. 1946.
2. ST. AUGUSTINE, THE FIRST CATECHETICAL INSTRUCTION. Trans. by Joseph P. Christopher, Ph.D. Pages vi + 176. 1946.
3. ST. AUGUSTINE, FAITH, HOPE, AND CHARITY. Trans. by Louis A. Arand, S.S., S.T.D. Pages vi + 165. 1947.
4. JULIANUS POMPERIUS, THE CONTEMPLATIVE LIFE. Trans. by Sr. Mary Josephine Suelzer, Ph.D. Pages vi + 220. 1947.
5. ST. AUGUSTINE, THE LORD'S SERMON ON THE MOUNT. Trans. by John J. Jepson, S.S., Ph.D. Pages vi + 227. 1948.
6. THE DIDACHE, THE EPISTLE OF BARNABAS, THE EPISTLES AND THE MARTYRDOM OF ST. POLYCARP, THE FRAGMENTS OF PAPIAS, THE EPISTLE TO DIOGNETUS. Trans. by James A. Kleist, S.J., Ph.D. Pages vi + 235. 1948.
7. ARNOBIUS, THE CASE AGAINST THE PAGANS, Vol. 1. Trans. by George E. McCracken, Ph.D. Pages vi + 372. 1949.
8. ARNOBIUS, THE CASE AGAINST THE PAGANS, Vol. 2. Trans. by George E. McCracken, Ph.D. Pages vi + 287. 1949.
9. ST. AUGUSTINE, THE GREATNESS OF THE SOUL, THE TEACHER. Trans. by Joseph M. Colleran, C.SS.R., Ph.D. Pages vi + 255. 1950.
10. ST. ATHANASIUS, THE LIFE OF SAINT ANTONY. Trans. by Robert T. Meyers, Ph.D. Pages vi + 155. 1950.
11. ST. GREGORY THE GREAT, PASTORAL CARE. Trans. by Henry Davis, S.J., B.A. Pages vi + 281. 1950.
12. ST. AUGUSTINE, AGAINST THE ACADEMICS. Trans. by John J. O'Meara, D.Phil. Pages vi + 213. 1950.
13. TERTULLIAN, TREATIES ON MARRIAGE AND REMARRIAGE: TO HIS WIFE, AN EXHORTATION TO CHASTITY, MONOGAMY. Trans. by William P. LeSaint, S.J., S.T.D. Pages viii + 194. 1951.
14. ST. PROSPER OF AQUITAINE, THE CALL OF ALL NATIONS. Trans. by P. De Letter, S.J., S.T.D. Pages vi + 234. 1952.
15. ST. AUGUSTINE, SERMONS FOR CHRISTMAS AND EPIPHANY. Trans. by Thomas C. Lawler. Pages vi + 249. 1952.
16. ST. IRENAEUS, PROOF OF THE APOSTOLIC PREACHING. Trans. by Joseph P. Smith, S.J. Pages viii + 233. 1952.
17. THE WORKS OF ST. PATRICK, ST. SECUNDINUS, HYMN ON ST. PATRICK. Trans. by Ludwig Bieler, Ph.D. Pages vi + 121. 1953.
18. ST. GREGORY OF NYSSA, THE LORD'S PRAYER, THE BEATITUDES. Trans. by Hilda C. Graef. Pages vi + 210. 1954.
19. ORIGEN, PRAYER, EXHORTATION TO MARTYRDOM. Trans. by John J. O'Meara, D.Phil. Pages viii + 253. 1954.
20. RUFINUS, A COMMENTARY ON THE APOSTLES' CREED. Trans. by J. N. D. Kelly, D.D. Pages viii + 166. 1955.